DEVELOPING
A TORAH
PERSONALITY

MOSAICA PRESS

DEVELOPING A TORAH PERSONALITY

PERSONALITY

Insights, Anecdotes & Wisdom for Life

AVRAHAM BOGOPULSKY

Mosaica Press, Inc.

© 2016 by Mosaica Press

Designed and typeset by Rayzel Broyde

ISBN-10: 1-937887-77-4

ISBN-13: 978-1-937887-77-3

Published and distributed by:

Mosaica Press, Inc.

www.mosaicapress.com

info@mosaicapress.com

לעילוי נשמת

ר׳ משה יצחק בן צבי לייב ז״ל
וצפורה בת שמעי״ה הלוי ז״ל

In memory of

Morrie and Barbara Steiman, z"l

who from day one supported and believed in

Rabbi Avraham and Rebbetzin Leah Bogopulsky

to lead and carry on the torch of Torah

at Beth Jacob Congregation

and who witnessed their selfless dedication

to grow a community and give 200 percent of themselves.

חני ויהודה לייב שטיימאן ומשפחתם

Dedicated by

Edward & Anita Bogopulsky

In honor of their

children, grandchildren and

great grandchildren

שיהיו עוסקים בתורה ובמצוות

❦

Dedicated by

Tzvi & Pessie Rosen

In honor of their

children, grandchildren and

great grandchildren

שיהיו עוסקים בתורה ובמצוות

Dedicated in honor of our

children, grandchildren,

great grandchildren and

future generations

RAPHAEL AND KITTY SILVERMAN

לְעִילוּי נִשְׁמַת

In loving memory of

Stacy Lynne Pariser

חיה ארוכה לאה בת יבלחט״א פסח שמעון

נלב״ע ח׳ אדר תשנ״ג

This *sefer* should inspire continued learning, teaching and
fulfilling of Hashem's Torah through the author.

PAUL S. PARISER AND FAMILY

לעילוי נשמת אחי הגדול

ר׳ יעקב אליעזר ז״ל

בן יבלחט״א ר׳ יהושע העשל

בוגופולסקי

נלב״ע כד׳ ניסן תשע״ה

תנצב״ה.

⌒•⌒

L'iluy Nishmas

Reb Yosef ben Reb Pinchas, z"l

Base Dina bas Reb Tzvi Zev, z"l

Reb Sender ben Reb Shlomo, z"l

Brachah and *hatzlachah* for Sidney and Yael Goldberg

Max and Sharon Goldberg

⌒•⌒

In memory of

Rachel and Yearl Schwartz, z"l

Their love of children and pursuit of kindness was their goal in life.

May they rest in peace.

Letters of Approbation

Rabbi Avraham Bogopulsky's book on Jewish life is full of insight, wisdom, and compassion. It is scholarly, yet practical, well-written, and without being preachy or overly academic, it conveys knowledge and depth. It deals squarely with the issues of life that all of us face and does so through the prism of Jewish tradition and the experience of decades of being a synagogue rabbi. Everyone will gain wisdom and insight in their lives from reading this book.

All blessings,
Berel Wein

All of us are frustrated. We face difficulties in our careers, businesses, social lives, and family relationships. We turn to the writings of religious teachers, hoping that they can give us authentic spiritual guidance. Although we find their advice erudite and scholarly, too often it is far removed from our everyday reality. Rarely do we read a book written by someone who is truly familiar with our mundane routines, compassionately empathetic with our daily dilemmas, and yet capable of finding practical, helpful, and inspiring solutions to our troubling questions in authentic Jewish sources.

Rabbi Bogopulsky's *Developing a Torah Personality* fits the bill! It abounds with anecdotes drawn from real life and articulates the questions which really bother us. The reader finds himself saying, "That's exactly what I'm going through!" The reader is then astounded by Rabbi Bogopulsky's ability to find sources in our tradition, sometimes going back centuries and also quoting from contemporary sages, which address real life issues. We frequently find ourselves in a wilderness of doubt, confusion, and despair. This book shows us paths out of that wilderness.

Congratulations, Rabbi Bogopulsky. Your book is a precious gift to all who seek practical wisdom from the Jewish tradition!

Rabbi Tzvi H. Weinreb

Living in an "out-of-town" Jewish community gives one a unique and different perspective of Jewish life in America. Serving as a rabbi in an "out-of-town" community provides unexpected challenges and unusual circumstances. The questions posed by the congregants are not the typical, What happens if I stir a cup of coffee with a meat spoon? The questions are more of a personal, social, and ethical nature. The answers are not easily found in the Talmud or codes of Jewish Law. In order to answer these questions requires a familiarity with Rabbinical works on Jewish philosophy and ethical matters. It is a whole new world out there and requires a very special sensitivity and area of expertise. The rabbi's sermon on Shabbos is not a homiletical exercise in Talmudic and Midrashic gymnastics, but rather it provides sweet words to live by. The rabbi serves as a knowing guide, blazing the trail through the wilds of Jewish America and the path leading to the World to Come.

Rabbi Avraham Bogopulsky chose to face these challenges head on. San Diego was not to be a rest stop on the way to a position in Brooklyn; it was a destination. For almost twenty years, Rabbi Bogopulsky has met the challenges and continues to inspire his congregation and the Jewish community at large. His reputation for his adherence to Jewish Law and his commitment to the shul has spread across America to the communities of Lakewood, Monsey, and Brooklyn. Of course, behind every rabbi is a rebbetzin who also serves the community and inspires her husband. As James Barrie wrote, "Every man who is high up likes to think he has done it all himself, and the wife smiles and lets it go at that." This description certainly befits Rebbetzin Leah Bogopulsky.

What is not always recognized is that the congregation also inspires the rabbi. They enable him to see insights in the Torah and the Talmud that, on his own, he might not have seen. The members of the congregation inspire the rabbi who, in turn, inspires them. It is all part of the Torah life cycle.

Rabbi Bogopulsky has compiled in book form a series of those mutually inspiring messages. Though it is deceivingly easy reading, it contains life-enhancing words. I am personally delighted that the Rabbi has allowed us to benefit from his insights.

May the Rabbi and his community continue on their path together for many more years to come.

Leibel Reznick
Monsey, New York

Table of Contents

Acknowledgments

n preparing the remarks for my book, I read many introductions of other authors and I must say I am very intimidated by this daunting task. Trying to capture everything and everyone is nearly impossible and therefore I state at the outset, if there is anyone who I left out, I apologize.

Hodu la'HaShem ki tov, ki le'olam chasdo. Thanks to *HaKadosh Baruch Hu* for giving me the strength, health, fortitude, and insights to bring this *sefer* to the world. The publication of a book is similar to giving birth to a child; I truly feel this way.

An often-asked question is, Where do I begin? I usually suggest starting from the beginning. As with many projects, they never start out with the intention that it actually ends on. I remember sitting in a *shiur* given by Rabbi Wein in yeshivah about thirty years ago. He explained the very simple words of *Pirkei Avos*, "*u'knei lecha chaver—* acquire a friend for yourself," as the friend being the pen. A person's thoughts become his friend, and through this message, Rabbi Wein encouraged us to write.

Fast-forward to about five years ago and Rabbi Wein's voice is ringing again, this time telling me that a shul rabbi has to write something about the *parashah* every week. I said to myself, *I will try and see how it goes.* I committed myself to one year, which extended to three, and now I and my friend are completing a five-year project. In it, my thoughts about daily living and ordinary events that we can all relate to are connected to the *parshiyos* of the week. Thank you, Rabbi Wein!

The book has taken on a life of its own through the efforts of the Mosaica Press team led by Rabbis Yaacov Haber and Doron Kornbluth.

After going through the process of publishing a book, I realized that a writer without a good team of editors is like a driver who doesn't have the directions. On a weekly basis I would send my work to an incredible, dedicated woman, who would always find the time to review and work out the kinks in my message. If it wasn't for Mrs. Elaine Lepow, I probably would have stopped writing a long time ago. Thank-you, Elaine, for all that you do, and especially for guiding and tweaking the weekly message. A second editor was added to view not the individual messages, but rather to edit the work as a book. Rabbi Eliyahu Friedman's insights and delicate understanding of my work helped shape and form the work as presented. Thank-you, Elaine and Eliyahu, for giving me those directions to get to the final destination.

I would like to thank my Rebbi, Rabbi Laibel Reznick, who has guided me and my family for the last thirty years. His deep knowledge and insight into Torah and life has truly shaped our family. Many of the *divrei Torah* and original thoughts you will read may seem a bit radical or nontypical. In addressing whether or not some ideas are kosher, I doubled checked with my Rebbi to make sure I quoted him correctly. He once said, "If a *peshat* or *dvar Torah* 'makes sense,' then it is *emes* and we can say it." All of the words presented here were all said by Moshe Rabbeinu, I have only reformatted them.

I cannot honestly say I learned something from all of my teachers, but from those whom I did learn, it was a lot. From the teacher who gave me the building blocks of learning the *alef-beis*—the foundation it all stands on—to the *rabbe'im* from yeshiva in Eretz Yisrael, to Yeshiva Shaarei Torah in Monsey, they gave me the *chizuk* and beauty of Torah.

I grew and gained from the communities of Binghamton, N.Y. and Charleston, S.C., where I developed skills in teaching Torah in day school and at the pulpit. The bulk of my developed skills and career came during the last eighteen years from my shul, Beth Jacob Congregation in San

Diego, C.A. Beth Jacob has afforded me the opportunity to grow and serve in this position. It has been a labor of love in teaching all levels and segments of the shul. The families of the shul are exactly that—family. The members of my shul have supported me in this endeavor and many others that have contributed to the spiritual growth of our community. Each and every one in the shul should live and be well, to read my articles every week.

To my parents, Edward and Anita Bogopulsky, and my in-laws, Pessi and Tzvi Rosen. The words "unconditional love" are truly a large part of their essence. I cannot think of any decision I made that they not only agreed to, but encouraged as well. Their financial and emotional support made this project reach fruition. They should continue to be blessed with future generations of grandchildren and great-grandchildren being *ovdei HaShem*. HaShem should bless them with *u'mi'kol tuv le'olam al yechasreinu*.

To my children Yehudis and Yaacov Kaplan; Yisrael and Malka Bogopulsky; Dovid and Malkie Bogopulsky; Hadassa and Jeremy Burg; and Aryeh Leib; and grandchildren Zevi, Raizy, and Miri Kaplan; Kayla and Rella Bogopulsky; and Ayala Bogopulsky—you are the reasons Ima and I keep on pushing. The *zechus* of this book should give you all *siyata di'Shemaya* to grow in Torah and *yir'as Shamayim*, and to raise the future *doros* of *bnei* and *bnos Torah*.

To my dear wife, Leah, thank-you for all the care and support. It is because of you and your multitasking capabilities at work, shul, and with our family that has given me the space and time to work on this *sefer*. Your investment in our family gives you more than half of the dividends that stem from this *limud haTorah*.

I hope you enjoy reading the lessons, parables, and words of Torah. My goal was to make you, the reader, feel the message was intended for you and not "the other guy." The ultimate purpose is not just to read it, but rather to be inspired and live the lessons that should make us all better Jews and shine as God's chosen people to the world, Amen!

Introduction

Literary works are often sought out by people looking for something worthwhile to read. The world today places so many demands upon us that reading has gone from an essential part of our day to a downright burden. Not so many years ago people typically read their favorite newspapers in the morning, enjoyed a weekly or monthly magazine as time permitted during the week, and curled up in bed with a good book in the evening. Today, most people read because they have to: either because of school, work, or because their parents make them.

Those who still read for recreation are asked, Was the book you just finished a good read or really great? Have you ever thought about what stands between a good book, something which was just enjoyable, and a truly great book? The difference may be that a good book is a diversion which may give pleasure while you are reading it; a great book, however, is uplifting. It brings you into the story so strongly that you do not want it to end. I recently finished a really great book—the story of Rabbi Israel Meir Lau, the former Chief Rabbi of Israel. I was upset when I finished it; his life story is riveting and the writing was wonderful. Every book needs a beginning and an end—even one so outstanding that the reader feels a sense of regret when he has reached the last page.

I recall my days in Yeshiva Shaarei Torah, listening to a shmooze given by my *rosh yeshivah*, Rabbi Berel Wein. Rabbi Wein frequently recommended books (secular, but kosher) for us to read. Usually these books were massive and very deep, making it difficult to keep up with the pace of his suggestions. He insisted that all of us read the newspaper in order to keep abreast of current events and emphasized that reading secular books would enhance and mold our approach to Judaism.

Tanach, which is an acronym for Torah, *Neviim*, and *Kesuvim*, are the three sections of twenty-four books which make up the Written Law. We are familiar with the first of these three: the Torah—the *Chamishah Chumshei Torah* or the Five Books of Moses. In *parashas Beha'alosecha* we are informed that there are really seven books, not five. In *Bamidbar*, two *pesukim* (10:35–36) are surrounded by two upside down (or inverted) *nuns*. The Gemara in *Shabbos* 116a explains that these two verses are actually an independent book, leading Rashi to say that the book of *Bamidbar* is really three books in one: one book before these *pesukim*, a second book consisting of these two *pesukim*, and a third book continuing after these two *pesukim*. If *Bamidbar* is actually three books, then we have a total of seven books from *Bereishis* through *Devarim*.

The Kli Yakar wonders how it is possible that these two verses actually make up an entire book. He asks, Where is there a mitzvah found in this two-verse *sefer*, since every one of the *sefarim* of the Torah should contain at least one mitzvah! Where is the mitzvah within these two sentences that comprise a book? He explains that HaShem made this book purely for the mitzvah of *peru u'revu* (to "be fruitful and multiply"). The world's continued existence is contingent upon this mitzvah. As it states in *Yevamos* 64a: "Whoever does not involve himself in this mitzvah of *peru u'revu* causes God's Presence to leave the Jewish people." It states in the second of these two *pesukim* (*Bamidbar* 10:36): "*U'venucho yomar shuva HaShem rivevos alfei Yisrael—Reside tranquilly, HaShem, among the myriads and thousands of Israel.*" The word *alfei* is the plural of "one thousand," so the minimum plural it could be is "two thousand," and the word "myriad" means "ten thousand," so the minimum "myriads" could mean is "twenty thousand," making it a total of twenty-two thousand adult men required for HaShem to rest within the Jewish people. Even one person not engaged in the proactive mitzvah of being fruitful and multiplying can adversely affect reaching this minimum requirement and will lead to the departure of HaShem's Presence. In *Bereishis*, God created man and immediately commanded him to be fruitful and multiply. The very first mitzvah given to the world through Adam was to try to have children, to procreate human beings who are created in the image of HaShem. If we turn away from this command, we are acting contemptibly, as if we do not value HaShem, so we don't have to obey His mandate. Nor are we showing any appreciation for the preciousness of people created in the image of God, thereby diminishing His greatness in the eyes of others.

This middle book of *Bamidbar*, consisting of only two *pesukim*, describes the mitzvah of *peru u'revu* and its implications. It stresses the magnitude of trying to have children and the consequences if we do not try. The direct implication of this mitzvah is that either HaShem's Presence joins us or leaves us.

It all focuses on creating a new human being to carry on and give inspiration to the world. It's true that people make up the world, but each person makes up the people. Every single individual carries the weight and meaning of this world, as it says in *Sanhedrin* 37a: "The world was created just for me."

A book of any size can make a great impact upon a person, especially if it is a great book. There are books that tell the stories of giants among men—people who have accomplished great feats despite the odds they faced and the adversity they struggled with in their lives. And there are books that focus on the value and importance of each of us, on the possibilities within us to add to the positive, to the good of this world.

A good book makes someone feel good; a great book motivates a person to become a better person, to make a better world. In addition to learning Torah, a person should read great books, books that inspire him to do more for his family, community, and the Jewish people. When I read the accomplishments of great people, I am stirred by the realization of how much more each of us is capable of accomplishing. I am motivated to try to do more.

The books of the Written Torah and the Oral Torah make up the framework for our lives, telling us how to live. There are inspiring people discussed in the Torah, though somewhat difficult to relate to. Reading a book about a contemporary giant gives us the tools and motivation to become greater people and ultimately serve our people by leading a life of greatness.

When my Rebbi, Rabbi Wein, completed his first book, he said he had some notion of what it must feel like to give birth to a child. Now, in retrospect, I may have a new understanding of that feeling. Our purpose in life is to help, inspire, create opportunities for people to advance spiritually, and give them the tools and means to grow in their *avodas HaShem*. Giving birth to a human being sets the stage for us to mold a child to do just that, to help the world. Through the dissemination of thoughts and lessons that are written in this book, I hope to accomplish the same thing.

Using my own life experiences and daily observations, I have tried to relate many of the lessons found in the Torah. I hope and pray that this book should not only be good, but rather great in the sense that the lessons and *divrei Torah* that are learned should give the reader inspiration and determination to seek a tighter bond with the One and Only—*HaKadosh Baruch Hu.*

A TIME TO LAUGH, A TIME TO CRY, AND
NOW IT'S TIME TO GET UP AND GO!

CHAPTER ONE
TIME

O ne of the timeless teachings a parent helps his child to master is how to tell time. I was blessed to be forced to learn how to tell time with an analog watch or clock. I was born in 1964, and as I was learning how to understand and read an analog watch, digital watches were beginning to appear in the stores.

The earliest U.S. patent for a digital alarm clock was registered to D.E. Protzmann and others on October 23, 1956. Protzmann and his associates also patented another digital clock in 1970 which was said to use a minimal amount of moving parts. Two side-plates held digital numerals between them, while an electric motor and cam gear outside controlled the movement. In 1970, the first digital wristwatch with an LED display was mass-produced. It was called the Pulsar and was produced by the Hamilton Watch Company. Throughout the 1970s, despite the initial hefty cost of digital watches, the popularity of those devices steadily rose.

Looking back, I was fortunate to have learned to read an analog watch instead of relying on a digital one. Many people today have difficulty making sense out of an analog clock. These individuals are often unable to tell time using a watch or clock without numbers or a second hand. Not everyone needs to become a horologist or learn to master a sundial, but everyone should learn the basics of telling time.

Perhaps more important than telling time is the art of *managing* one's time in order to make the most of it. When you think about it, there is little reason to know the time if you do not try to manage it better!

Today, shuls across the globe have digital clocks situated in strategic positions throughout the sanctuary for a host of different reasons. The four primary reasons I would venture to list are:

- To assure the davening starts on time;
- To facilitate the recitation of *Kerias Shema* prior to the latest time permitted in the morning;
- Simply to know what time it is;
- To enable the congregants to track exactly how much time the rabbi's *derashah* took.

Despite the popular use of the digital clock in shuls today, there is perhaps a conceptual advantage to the dial of the analog clock. The second hand (the second counter) goes around once and then the minute hand moves one little notch to the right, while the digital seconds actually count from zero to fifty-nine over and over again. The ceaseless progression of the numbers makes one more aware of the actual ticking away of real time.

Time is one of the most precious commodities we have, yet it is always uncontrollably and steadily decreasing—when we have to get somewhere or do something or how much longer we will live. This is a frightening thought. In *Shemos* 12:2 the Torah states: "*Ha'chodesh ha'zeh lachem rosh chadashim rishon hu lachem l'chadshei ha'shanah—This month will be first of all the months; it will be the first to you of the months of the year.*" Rav Ovadia ben Yaakov Sforno, in his commentary on Chumash, explains the significance of the word *lachem* ("to you") in the *pasuk*.

The process of *yetzias Mitzrayim* ("the Exodus from Egypt") can be said to have had different stages of development. One of these stages was the completion of the Ten Plagues, whereby the land of Egypt was decimated and the Egyptians' ability to keep the Jews enslaved was marginal. I heard Dr. David Pelcovitz quote from the Maharal that a sign of slavery is the lack of time an individual has for himself. Therefore, immediately after the warning that there would be one more *makkah*, the slaying of the firstborn was proclaimed. The Jewish people were now on the threshold of entering a new dimension of time: transcending from perceiving time as slaves to perceiving time as free men. From this point on, the months would belong *la'chem* ("to you"), in order for you to be free to utilize your time. During the period of slavery, the days—and time itself—did not belong to the Jewish people, but rather to others; time was used at the whim and will of their oppressors.

This was the beginning of the reality of free choice and the decision-making process of how to manage our own time. In order for a person to have free will, he needs to have free time. The prerequisite of the Jews accepting the Torah was to have control over their own space and time. In order to fulfill a mitzvah, a person needs the time to do it. One of the obstacles that makes it difficult for Jews to fulfill and observe mitzvos is the *yetzer hara* filling up our free time with non-essential, trivial matters. Although everyone needs a break and, thus, downtime is an important and necessary component in our *avodas HaShem* ("service of God"), nevertheless, we all are guilty of wasting an enormous amount of time with mundane activities that really do not help us.

We need to calculate our time and make sure it is used efficiently and wisely. The clock of life does not stop for even one second. Every second that passes us will never come back. If we did not use the time we were given judiciously, we are guilty of wasting that precious commodity. Life is too short; we need to appreciate every moment and use time wisely.

The most critical component of time management is knowing how to tell time. Whether the clock is analog or digital is really not so important. Appreciating every tick of the clock and making it count— one second at a time—is an essential part of wisdom.

◆ ◆ ◆

How much do we contemplate the amount of time spent in our lifetime just waiting? Whether it is waiting in line at the grocery store or sitting in the waiting room of a doctor's office, the time spent waiting can be excessively long. I recently had a three o'clock appointment with a certain professional and did not actually see the person until twenty minutes after four. Many thoughts crossed my mind: should I get up and leave, ask what's taking so long, or just continue to be patient and wait? While mulling this situation over, I thought of so many other times we are put into situations where we just wait for long periods of time, reacting differently each time depending upon the situation and our mood.

While driving, we frequently find ourselves in heavy traffic or stopped by a red light that seems like it will never turn green. There are times when we have the patience to put up with these delays, but there are other times our patience runs extremely thin.

Why does our level of tolerance vary from one situation to another? It usually depends upon how much we want or need that which we are waiting for. There is a certain experience some of you may have had waiting to receive a *berachah* from a Chasidic Rebbe. I remember all too well waiting to see the Skverer Rebbe on a Thursday night. We arrived around ten o'clock and did not see the Rebbe until about two-thirty in the morning. Yet despite the wait, there was great anticipation in seeing a holy man such as the Skverer Rebbe.

The irony of waiting is clear: for something that we look forward to, peacefulness reigns; but waiting for something that we dread can feel like awaiting a death sentence. There was a joke someone told in yeshivah many years ago describing the length of a class. For a tzaddik ("a righteous person"), attending and listening to a *shiur* ("class") is Gan Eden ("paradise"), but for an evil person, listening to that same class is an eternal sentence to Gehinnom ("purgatory"). Everybody views waiting for things differently.

A question was once asked to the Gerrer Rebbe. The Gemara in *Sanhedrin* 97 states: "The son of David (Mashiach) will not come until we give up hope of ever being redeemed." Yet we, the Jewish people, never give up hope, as we recite daily one of the Thirteen Principles of Maimonidies: "We believe with perfect faith in the coming of Mashiach... and even though he may delay, nevertheless I anticipate every day that he will come." So if we never give up hope as we wait every day, how will Mashiach ever come in deference to the Gemara in *Sanhedrin*?

The Gerrer Rebbe quipped and said, "If this is what we think, that Mashiach won't come because we remember him, then there is no greater despair than that!" There is no question we must never stop thinking that Mashiach will come, and more accurately, in our very time.

Many people today are constantly worried and can end up in a mode of anticipating the bad. They occupy their minds with the pessimistic prospects of how this might go wrong or how this might not materialize. Sometimes this can entail long-term stretches of distress. Although a healthy dosage of concerning yourself with avoiding negative results can be essential to success in all endeavors, nevertheless, worrying as a pattern of thought never produces a positive accomplishment. The time wasted just waiting for the negative results to happen actually contribute to the negativity of the world. On the other hand, waiting for something good creates an anticipation of hope and promise for the future. As long as we wait for the good, the potential is great; how much more so when the good actually comes about. This is cause for great celebration.

The challenge for us today is, What do we do during these recurring waiting periods that we find ourselves in? Do we use the time effectively and wisely, or do we waste it chasing frivolous adventure that gains us nothing—not in this world and not in the next? We are all aware of the precious gift of time. The clock can never be turned back. Priceless moments are given to us in life that we should not allow to slip away without proper attention.

Let us intelligently use the time that we wait for a blessing from a tzaddik, or to see a health professional, or even something more mundane like waiting at the check-out counter at the grocery store, and make it more meaningful. This seeming "gap" in our day is actually a wonderful opportunity to accomplish. Call someone who needs a *refuah sheleimah*, learn some Mishnayos, or be creative in your own way to turn the waiting into something positive.

◆　◆　◆

One of the obstacles some *baalei teshuvah* experience is that they learn to read quickly! Typically when a person begins to read Hebrew, the effort of decoding causes him to read very slowly. As he becomes more proficient in his reading skills, he tends to speed up, becoming increasingly fluent orally. With this growing skill, his davening is transformed from reading with care, making sure to decode each syllable correctly (good), to reading at rocket speed (bad).

Perhaps one of the fastest readings we ever hear in shul is from *parashas Naso*—the repetition of the offerings the *Nesiim* ("tribal leaders") brought at the time of the inauguration of the Mishkan. Each *Nasi* brought the identical set of animals for his sacrifice. Due to this fact, the series of seven verses is repeated no less than twelve times. The *baal koreh*, the reader, often reads it very fast. People don't seem to be interested in hearing the same thing over and over, and he is very familiar with the words and the cantillation, and therefore can speed through it. It is, however, an official disgrace to the Torah to zip through these seven verses over and over.

Reb Yitzchak Meir Alter, the Chidushei HaRim, explains the repetition of the offerings in a completely different light. In *Bamidbar* 7:18–19, the Torah states: "*On the second day, Nesanel ben Tzuar, leader of Yissachar, brought his offering: one silver bowl, its weight 130 shekels; and one silver basin of 70 shekels in the sacred shekel; both of them filled with fine flour mixed with oil for a meal offering.*" Rashi tells us the numerical value of the words *kaaras kesef*, the silver bowl, equals 930, matching the years of Adam HaRishon's life. The Chidushei HaRim asks, Why did Rashi only start explaining the reasons for the sacrifices of the second day and not mention anything of the first day's offerings of *Shevet Yehuda*?

The Chidushei HaRim answers as follows: There is no question that there was a good reason that Nachshon brought sacrifices for the tribe of Yehuda on the first day. With regard to the tribe of Yissachar, however, one might think that Nesanel only brought offerings on the second day to follow in like manner the tribe that brought them first! Therefore Rashi comes to inform us that Nesanel brought offerings on the second day for his own reasons—completely independent of Nachshon. *Midrash Rabbah* 13:14 explains in detail why each *Nasi* decided to bring sacrifices. One idea it proposed was that the *Nesiim* brought an offering for different chapters in the history of the world and cites stories from the time of Creation until the building of the Mishkan to support this view. To illustrate, if the second day represented Adam's life span, the first day represented the creation of the world itself. The third *Nasi* was from Zevulun, who was a merchant on the high seas. This is representative of the *teivah*, the ark that Noach built to save the world. This continued for all the offerings up until the time of the Mishkan. The *korbanos* of each tribal leader had great significance and personal meaning to each of those who offered them.

The final *Nasi* was Achira ben Einan from the tribe of Naftali. Since he was a *ben einan*, a *tov ayin*—a good eye—he was selected to go last. He did not cast an evil eye upon the others who had gone before him. To the contrary, Achira ben Einan had a good eye for all the colleagues who went before him. Even though he went last, it did not detract from his positive attitude; he only saw the good in all of his colleagues. Perhaps he also saw the advantage of going last; he did not feel pressured to finish quickly, thinking someone else still needed to go. This is another sublime message for going slow: take the time to look at things that you never get a chance to see, feel, hear, smell, or touch.

I remember traveling on the New York City subway, noticing the difference between the local and express lines. Anyone who has ever been on a speeding train can remember that everything viewed through the window is just a blur. As the train starts to slow down, more and more comes into focus. This analogy directly relates back to why we need to read each part of the Torah slowly. Even though we think we know what is being read, our understanding does not begin to scratch the surface.

Truth be told, everything in life has a greater beauty and more inner meaning than we are able to see from the surface. When it comes to our relationship with HaShem, we need to slow down, take our time, and not be in such a rush. Every word of davening has many meanings and interpretations that we need to digest in order to handle different situations and challenges in life. If we continue to say the *tefillos* in an identical manner each and every day—only faster—then we are blocking our ability to conceive of possible aid that we may need. If we are rushing to work and just mumble good morning and quickly glance at the person we are passing, we have robbed ourselves of potentially seeing the other side of that person. If we do not take the time to sit down and talk with our loved ones, but are always on the go, then we will never come to really know, understand, and appreciate them.

One of the great Chasidic masters taught that life has a starting and an ending point. The faster we go, the faster we get to the finish line. We should not be in a rush to reach the finish line before our time. When we read the portion about the *Nesiim*, the longest *parashah* of the year, as well as the other *parshiyos*, let us slow down—not just to think about the multiple messages that are being conveyed to us in these readings, but also to teach us a valuable lesson. We should strive to slow our lives down in order to truly appreciate the messages we receive each and every day from HaShem, and in order to more deeply appreciate the beauty and preciousness of the life we have been given.

◆ ◆ ◆

While we would like to slow down, the truth is that we live in a fast-paced world that too often forces us to do things quickly. So often we may feel the need to take a shortcut and do things not according to the book, just to get through the day. Unfortunately, the reality is quite the opposite. Whatever time you think you are saving will sooner or later cost you somewhere else. To our chagrin, the blame for this way of life is not always our own fault. The blame lies with a society that drives us to think, act, and react in a hasty, unthinking manner.

Two poignant examples come to mind, both of which occurred recently. The shul's office has a small refrigerator that holds small items for the staff. The fridge has a small freezer section that is not frost-free. It requires manual defrosting the old-fashioned way, by taking out all the food and leaving the unit unplugged so that the ice will melt, making a mess. Well, the *chacham* ("wise person") that I am decided this method takes too long and requires too much effort. Instead I decided to take a letter opener (why bother using a real ice pick...and who has one of those anyway?) and chop away at the ice to break it up. I was actually very successful. It took me remarkably less time, except for the small detail that was unbeknown to me: I punctured the cooling line and effectively broke the entire fridge!

A second episode occurred while preparing for Shabbos. I was in a hurry and quickly grabbed a bag containing two cartons of eggs, both of which proceeded to fall to the ground, leaving me with only one surviving carton of eggs. The amount of time it took to clean up the now slithery mass of broken eggs and go back to the store to buy more eggs was certainly longer than it would have taken to carefully handle the original bag.

Why do we sometimes act in rushed, irrational, unthinking ways? Experts will tell you that our behaviors may be caused by many different reasons, but I have found that when a person is physically tired, mentally strained, or just zinging out of focus, he is likely to do brash things that usually end up causing more damage than good.

We see this idea in the Torah itself. The Torah states in *Vayikra* 4:1: "*Daber el B'nei Yisrael laymor, nefesh ki secheta bi'shgagah mi'kol mitzvos HaShem asher lo sei'asena v'asa mei'achas meiheina—HaShem spoke to Moshe saying, 'Speak to the Children of Israel, saying: When a person will sin unintentionally from among all the commandments of HaShem that may not be done, and he will commit from one of them.'*" The Alshich HaKadosh explains the nature of sin through this verse. The aim of the Torah is that if a person sins accidentally, he should not say "How could I have done that sin?" Furthermore, even if he admits to wanting to commit that particular act, the sin was not done with the purpose of rebelling against HaShem, Heaven forbid.

When a person sins without *daas*—knowledge or consciousness or awareness—it's a sign that something is wrong with his/her *nefesh*. It is possible that this sin was committed due to a foreign thought that was only contemplated in the person's heart. The Alshich suggests that it was a previous sin or the thought of a sin that brought the person to sin accidentally now. If not for the commission of some previous transgression, it would not be possible to come to sin accidentally.

We know of a similar principle that says that HaShem does not give the animals of tzaddikim the opportunity to sin. How much more so would God not allow a *takalah*—a mistake—to come upon their owners, who are the actual righteous individuals. The concept of the animal not sinning (for example, not eating from grain that was not tithed properly) is the idea in this *pasuk*. But where do we see this idea of a previous sin triggering *"the soul that sins accidentally"*? It comes from the end of the *pasuk* that says *"and he will commit from one of them,"* that is, from all of the commandments that he did not violate, *but* he did do one of them! As a result of doing one *lo taaseh* ("do not do" commandment), this is the cause of his sinning *b'shogayg*, committed inadvertently again.

The general rule being proposed is if the soul of a person remains pure, there is less chance he will sin in the first place. But once the soul sins, a precedent has been set, establishing a platform for other sins to be committed, even without awareness. This *tumah*—impurity—makes it easier to commit another sin. Now we can understand the principle of *aveirah goreres aveirah*—one sin causes another sin.

In his introduction to *Vayikra*, the Abarbanel, Rabbi Don Isaac, writes that HaShem wanted to warn His children not to sin in front of Him and not to violate any of His commandments. Since we are only human and are therefore susceptible to sinning, HaShem gave us the opportunity to rid ourselves of physical, or worse, spiritual punishment by requesting a *korban* ("animal sacrifice") that is only a monetary punishment, so that our *neshamos* could remain as pure as possible in order not to get into the habit of sinning.

Why would anyone choose to make a mistake, causing himself grief and extra work? Why would anyone choose to sin, knowing the consequences of his actions? People make poor choices when their guard is down, perhaps due to fatigue, irritability, or just being in a rush. Whether these are done in the physical world or in the spiritual world, the reasons and causes can be traced back to the same issues.

Let us all slow down and think before we act.

Let's add a companion thought to the quote from Benjamin Franklin that "haste makes waste": thinking with deliberation can prevent aggravation.

◆　◆　◆

How fast do you eat?

When it comes to eating out, people choose between fine dining and fast food joints. A fine dining experience will usually take a few hours...to eat food that can typically be eaten in a few minutes. A few weeks ago, I ate in a restaurant with an all-you-can-eat menu in Israel. The experience was gluttonous—they served seven different types of meats, chicken, and a plethora of side dishes. Diners were invited to taste as many of these delicacies as they wished. There was no time limit; you could stay there for six hours, get up and walk around, etc. There is a distinct feeling of royalty when surrounded with the lavishness of eating in an environment of opulence. However, the blunt reality is that this indulgence borders on the prohibition of excessive eating, a negative commandment in the Torah.

Ironically, on the other hand, this feast engendered a feeling of satiation whereby I might have been obligated to recite the full *Birkas HaMazon* despite not having eaten any bread. This culinary experience promoted dining with a sense of ease and relaxation, which maximized enjoying and savoring every taste sensation. In a typical setting, one would not take the time to appreciate the full flavor of meat and other fine foods attained by eating slowly. I would rather, for example, opt to indulge in a good rib steak by swiftly consuming it.

Although a Jewish lifestyle does not afford the time for, let alone approve of, a preoccupation with magnifying our enjoyment of food, eating quickly is not necessarily a virtue either. Eating too fast can wreak havoc on the intestinal tract. Chewing properly and ingesting normal amounts are healthy habits. Every dietician, doctor, and health professional will tell you that eating slowly helps your digestion, keeps your weight in check, and helps to contribute to a more enjoyable lifestyle. There are always exceptions, but this should be the norm.

Interestingly, when it comes to communal or private prayer, a person develops habits regarding the way he davens that are very similar to his development of habits in the way he eats. A person doesn't realize that his body adapts to a certain routine—whether when eating or davening. After a period of time, a person can and will adapt to a new environment, particularly with regard to speed of davening, and will tend to daven at the pace of those around him. This is especially true when we find ourselves in an environment which is different from that which we are accustomed to, going from fast to slow and vice versa. Someone who is used to davening quickly will, at times, find himself in a slower minyan. Similarly, a person who typically eats quickly may be forced to eat slowly.

We have already established the fact that doing things slowly vis-à-vis eating is healthier: good sense will make the same case for davening. During the busy workweek a person may not have time to eat properly or to daven slowly for that matter. Nevertheless, when the opportunity to slow down occurs, we should take advantage of that time and enjoy it. This opportunity presents itself every week on Shabbos. Shabbos meals do not have to be rushed. We can enjoy the food, ambiance, and company during the Shabbos meals. In addition, the *tefillos* on Shabbos should be viewed as an invitation to take in all that prayer has to offer.

Just as we can sit down and savor a great meal by eating slowly, taking pleasure in every aspect of the meal, and giving it time to digest, so too can we use our mouths to savor the taste of the prayers. We have a chance to daven slowly, to think about the words and the meaning of the *tefillos* in a way that we may not have the chance to do during the week. It definitely requires a change of mindset to impact our approach to eating, and *kal va'chomer* ("how much more so") for davening.

Stop and think for a moment. Do we want to eat our words by half chewing or chewing so quickly that we devour them without even tasting them? Take the time to daven slowly and with greater *kavanah*—concentration and understanding—of the *tefillos*.

Hopefully, by eating slowly on Shabbos, we can try to train ourselves to eat a little slower during the week. Healthy eating habits contribute to becoming physically healthier. In the same vein we should enjoy and actually treasure slower davening on Shabbos. Hopefully, that too will carry over to our davening during the week, whether it's on a Sunday or a day off from work when we have more time.

◆ ◆ ◆

Life is so fast-paced today that we need to make sure to recharge our batteries. In fact, one of the diseases that plagues our society is the explosion of electronic devices. It is difficult to find a person who is not connected to some electronic device. Whether a laptop, Kindle, iPhone, Blackberry, iPad, Android, or just an ordinary cell phone, everyone's "hooked." We need to become concerned not only with electronic battery life, but with recharging our personal "batteries."

This notion of being plugged in was reinforced this week when I did some traveling. In today's day and age we rate airports not necessarily by how many eateries and restrooms there are, but rather if free Wi-Fi and plentiful charge stations are available. I have actually witnessed passengers go into a panic as their battery levels became critically low. One of the biggest selling points of most electronic devices is battery life. It is reasonable to expect that kinds of batteries and their chargeable life will increase as the auto industry paves the way for electric and battery-operated vehicles. Everyone knows the feeling when their devices are "dead" and the battery needs a charge or at least a life-sustaining rescue by being plugged in. We try to get as much of a battery charge as we can at an airport gate prior to boarding, delaying our "pulling the plug" to the last possible moment.

A few times a year my physical energy batteries become totally depleted. My body completely drains as a result of dehydration, lack of sleep, etc. In fact, my body gets so tired that my muscles and bones ache, and I literally cannot get out of bed. The body is an amazing machine that continuously dictates its needs. It will just shut down when its energy levels drop to a minimum. When this happens, I need to recharge by drinking huge amounts of fluids and getting a few hours of rest.

There is more of a connection between the physical and the spiritual than we may realize. In fact, the connection between the physical and the spiritual is one of the deepest connections that exists. In *Vayikra* 19:2, the Torah states: "*Daber el kal adas B'nei Yisrael v'amarta aleihem kedoshim tihiyu, ki kadosh Ani HaShem Elokeichem—Speak to the congregation of the children of Israel and say to them: You shall be holy, because I, HaShem your God, am holy.*" Rav Moshe Shternbuch, in his commentary *Taam VeDaas*, explains this verse by explaining the *Midrash Rabbah* 24:9 in *Vayikra*: "*Kedoshim tiheyu* ('*You shall be holy*')...*do you think you will be holy like Me, says God, because I am holy? My holiness is greater than your holiness!*"

Rav Shternbuch explains that the holiness of God is entirely spiritual, since God has no connection to physicality. Although God's holiness is only spiritual, He wants us, as physical beings, to emulate His holiness. The words "*because I am holy*" express a holiness which is exclusive to HaShem and *not* to humankind. Thus, the words "*to be holy*" were given to the Jewish people to be holy *as human beings*! We are commanded to sanctify ourselves mainly through the physical and mundane parts of our lives. HaShem wants us to be holy when we eat, when we drink, when we sleep, even when we talk and walk; we should be holy regarding everything and anything that is physical.

Other religions emphasize divesting from the physical world in order to attain a higher spiritual state. While other nations practice varying methods of estrangement from society, we, the Jewish people, require the company of others in order to raise the level of *kedushah*. It is the coming together of Jews and forming a united entity which so beautifully fulfills HaShem's will. This idea of coming together with fellow Jews is not limited to those Jews who follow the mitzvos; it includes violators of the Torah's laws as well. In the same vein that HaShem wants to get close to those who are "off the *derech*" through their repentance, so too we should get close to our nonobservant fellow Jews through outreach and helping them do mitzvos, as well.

Our physical batteries recharge through eating healthy food, exercise, and rest. Our spiritual batteries continually recharge through the performance and fulfillment of mitzvos. As we fulfill the mitzvos, we receive a stronger signal from the main station, HaShem. Everyone should realize that while performing mitzvos one may become physically tired and drained, but each of us continuously recharges our spiritual battery with this.

The one major difference between recharging our physical battery versus recharging our spiritual battery is that there is always a spiritual power source available. The opportunity for spiritual recharging requires no plug or outlet. A Jew can be any place in the world and still stay connected. By doing the right thing, he receives an automatic charge. We are made of batteries which have lifetime guarantees. They will always charge up if we spiritually try to connect ourselves to the source—HaShem and His Torah.

◆　◆　◆

Typically, summers offer us the chance to recharge our batteries— both spiritual and physical. It is a good time to take a break. In fact, summertime is associated with vacations and traveling. As I watched my children leave for camp, my childhood breaks came to mind. I then came to the realization that children's vacations are quite different from adult vacations. A child's vacation is a mental break from studying and learning in a formal school setting. Physically speaking, they get a chance to play more ball, swim, exercise, and the like. Adults also take physical and mental breaks, but with a different outcome at the end of the vacation.

In our day and age there are questions of protocol as to whether an employer may contact an employee while on vacation. Should employees be forced to take their smart phones or other portable devices with them in order to be available via e-mail, text messages, and the like? For me, getting ready to leave for vacation is stressful due to all the preparations and planning required for coverage during my absence. Furthermore, I am already beginning to transition from "being away" to "coming back" on the way to the airport or on the long drive home. Perhaps the days away are a physical rest, but they are not necessarily a mental vacation.

I often hear comments (mainly from myself) after a grueling trip that I need a vacation from my vacation. Physically speaking, I am indeed tired, but the truth is that often most of us push hard and don't get enough sleep. Creating a complete mental break and allowing our minds to be cleared from the stress of work is not an easy thing to accomplish. Some suggestions for a real mental vacation would be a change of scenery, getting fresh air, walking, and learning different parts of the Torah that we usually do not get a chance to learn.

Vacations are important, yet we need to make that downtime fruitful and beneficial. A trip or vacation must be planned carefully so that we maximize the downtime, enjoying both a physical and mental break, while endeavoring to build our spiritual beings. A vacation is never a break from spiritual growth; there is *no such thing* as a spiritual vacation. In fact, a vacation should *create* spiritual growth.

Toward the end of *Bamidbar* 33:1, the Torah states: "*Eileh maasei B'nei Yisrael asher yatzu mei'Eretz Mitzrayim l'tzivosam b'yad Moshe v'Aharon—These are the sojournings of the Children of Israel who left the land of Egypt with their hosts in the hands of Moshe and Aharon.*" Many of the commentaries ask why it was necessary to describe the travels of the Jewish people during their forty years in the desert. There are two important reasons why these details were given.

The first was for the "benefit of the body." The land of Egypt was a very good land. The Torah describes Egypt as "*k'gan HaShem k'Eretz Mitzrayim*" (the land of Egypt was like HaShem's garden), and the Jews related how fish there was both plentiful and inexpensive. The land of Israel, on the other hand, was still a developing country and not yet offering the material attractions of an established place. If the Jewish people would have immediately gone to Canaan from Egypt, they would not have been able to handle the contrast and transition. Therefore, HaShem, in His mercy, diverted the Jews for forty years, giving them time to forget about Egypt, letting the generation who left Egypt die out, and starting anew with a new generation.

The second reason was spiritual. The Midrash states that the Jews needed to travel in the desert so that the Torah they received on Har

Sinai would begin to set in their hearts and souls. Torah is something foreign to someone who has never been exposed to it. Wandering in the desert provided time for the Jewish people to get used to it by keeping the mitzvos and by learning Torah over and over again. The *baalei mussar* teach that when a person does something many times, it becomes *hergel*—he gets used to it and it becomes a part of him. By keeping the mitzvos and following the Torah for forty years, practicing Judaism became very natural for the B'nei Yisrael. Learning, teaching, and training oneself to be God-fearing became second nature. If they had entered immediately, they would have focused primarily on tending to their land, the vineyards, and the olive groves. Therefore HaShem diverted them and trained them in the important spiritual foundations prior to their having to deal with the physical side of living.

The end of the first *pasuk* mentions *"by the hand of Moshe and Aharon."* It is Moshe and Aharon, the leaders and teachers of the Jewish people, who set the tone and standards for the nation. It was they who taught the Jewish people about the *kedushah* of Eretz Yisrael—the holiness of the land—in order to work it properly. It was Moshe and Aharon who taught the Jews how to become a holy nation among the other nations and to lead by example.

The number forty rings out in other areas of the Torah, such as forty *seah* of the *mikveh* waters that purify us from impurity. It was forty days that Moshe was on Har Sinai in preparation for the giving of the Torah to Am Yisrael. The Jewish people needed forty years to get ready and "pack" the necessary items for their new life in Eretz Yisrael.

The Jewish people were vacating space and time within their own minds in transitioning from Mitzrayim to Eretz HaKedoshah, Eretz Yisrael. Physically, mentally, and spiritually, they were prepared by Moshe and Aharon.

We treasure the teachings of Moshe and Aharon, never leaving them behind when we go on vacation. The mental preparations we make prior to taking a vacation help us to live our lives as better, more dedicated Jews. The opportunity presented by a vacation which allows us to focus on spiritual growth will enrich and regenerate us when we return home.

IT IS OFTEN EASIER TO LEARN THE
ENTIRE TALMUD THAN TO CHANGE ONE
MIDDAH OR PERSONAL ATTRIBUTE.

(RABBI YISRAEL SALANTER)

CHAPTER TWO
HABITS

An interesting—and really chilling—phenomenon occurring more frequently as I get older is my repeating of lines that I hear from my elders. At certain times and in certain situations I was told "just wait until you're my age" and I scoffed at the idea; but now it has become the grim reality as I find myself saying and doing those same things!

One notable example is my trying to sleep late on Shabbos morning. Many older people who no longer must rise early encounter a challenge as they continue to wake up early. They may say to themselves "the morning after I retire from work I'm going to sleep in," only to find out that they still wake up at the same time they did for the last fifty years!

On Shabbos morning, the davening is later than during the week, and even though I do not have to get up early, I still wake up at the same time I do during the week. What is the force that causes me to rouse even when I have the luxury of sleeping later? The answer to this question is, of course, found in the Torah. *Vayikra* 26:3 states: "*Im be'chukosai teileichu v'es mitzvosai tishmiru va'asisem osam*—If in My statutes you go, and safeguard My commandments and perform them.*" The word *im*—if—is the key point.

The *Midrash Rabbah* quotes a verse from *Tehillim* 119:59: "*Chishavti derachai va'ashivah raglai el eidosecha*—I considered my ways and I turned *my feet toward Your testimonies.*" The thought in my brain sends a message to my feet to walk to the good places, such as shul and school, to learn Torah, and to follow in HaShem's ways. If a person does this repeatedly, then his body becomes accustomed to doing something consistently. After doing something hundreds or thousands of times—over and over again—it becomes second nature, and eventually the body just follows through on its own. With regularity, a person trains himself to act a certain way. This regularity will influence his body even when it tries to do something different.

Rav Eliyahu Dessler *zt"l* explains *Sukkah* 52a with this concept in mind. The Gemara states that in the future, families will cry in groups, men crying with men and women crying with women. They will cry because the men and the women were separated. Despite the fact that the evil inclination will no longer be present to create the urge for men and women to want to be together, they will cry *as if* this inclination is still there and wants them to be together with the opposite gender. That, however, will only be a residual memory of them wanting to be together during their lifetimes. Even without the presence of the evil inclination in the next world, they still want to sin because they became accustomed to the urge.

Another example is found in the Gemara in *Gittin* 57a, where Bilaam the *rasha*, even after leaving this world, was still trying to convince Onkelos not to convert to Judaism. Another story is related in *Sanhedrin* 63b. There the Jews were willing to give up their lives in order to serve idolatry. A young boy was close to death and Eliyahu HaNavi told the boy to recite the Shema and he would be saved! The boy refused, took out his little idol and kissed it, and then died upon it. The Gemara asks, How could such a thing happen? It answers that after the child became accustomed to believing that the idol was his god, it became a part of his soul. He could not give it up. Habits are, indeed, powerful.

On the positive side, we read stories of Jewish children taken into Catholic orphanages during the Holocaust who were identified after reciting the Shema at bedtime. They were conditioned to recite the Shema before going to bed and, even in a Catholic orphanage, this bedtime ritual stayed with them. As the rabbi who was searching for

Jewish children entered the orphanage, he started reciting the Shema very loudly and it struck a chord in the children. Without hesitating, they joined him in saying it and were taken back into Jewish custody.

My personal experience has been that it's easier to break a good habit than a bad one. In order to strengthen a good habit, a person has to put a lot of time and effort and repetitiveness into what he is doing. A bad habit, on the other hand, is difficult to break even if one has not been doing it for such a long time.

Another proof of the strength and influence of *hergel*—a repetitive behavior—is smoking or drinking. At first a person coughs from the smoke or chokes on the whiskey. After a while, however, he becomes used to it and dependent upon it, until he reaches the point where he cannot control it. Nevertheless, Rabbi Yehoshua ben Levi states in *Pirkei Avos* 6:2, "*The only free person is someone who is involved with and toils in the study of Torah.*" A person who constantly learns Torah has the ability to break a bad habit once he knows it's no good.

A person who woke up at five in the morning his entire adult life will continue to do so because his body is programmed and conditioned to rise then. This is the way his body works. Every one of us has many good and also some bad habits. The benefit an observant Jew has is the regiment of following the Torah. We have a *seder ha'yom*—an order to our days—a code of Jewish laws to follow. If and when we start to follow it, our bodies become conditioned to do the good things over and over again without even thinking about the effort they may entail.

Our challenge is putting in the time and effort that are necessary to make it habitual. Areas that we find we are lax in present opportunities. If we commit ourselves to taking on an improved behavior and give it an honest try to do it consistently for a while, it will eventually become second nature. We are always developing habits, good and bad. We all have the ability to develop good ones.

❖ ❖ ❖

I love baseball. Many people feel that baseball is boring. Quite the opposite! Aside from enjoying watching the actual game, there are many other facets and quirks unique to baseball. It is absorbing to see batters go through a series of preparations before they get up to bat... and most particularly when they are at the bat. In between pitches they readjust their gear, be it their helmets or batting gloves, or they reposition themselves in the batter's box.

Perhaps we can cite some examples of analogous conduct in one who is striving to stay focused in prayer. He too might need to readjust his "equipment." I find myself rewinding the tefillin on my arm, checking to make sure the tefillin on my head are centered, and constantly refolding my tallis over my shoulders.

Every person has his own unique routine and idiosyncrasies when it comes to davening. The actual place where a person prays, his particular *makom*—where he sits in the shul itself—is also part of the routine.

Some players get up to bat in a very nonchalant manner, and it is three swings and they're out. Some people take three steps back after the Shemoneh Esrei, and they're out! The Mishnah in *Berachos* relates how the earlier Chasidim used to pray nine hours a day: three hours for each prayer service. Each *tefillah* took three hours: one hour of preparation, one hour of prayer itself, and one hour of reflection after davening. The best athletes (*le'havdil bein kodesh l'chol!*) today put in a great deal of effort, not only during the game but in preparing for the game. Then, after the game they review the good and the bad of how the game went.

The key to success in both of these realms is consistency—doing the same thing day in and day out. It may seem boring, but routine is one of the major keys to success. One of the Torah sources for this is from the story of the Flood. There it proclaims, "*All flesh corrupted its ways on the land.*" The Beis HaLevi, in *parashas Noach*, explains that when a person repeats an *aveirah* ("sin"), we say "*hergel naaseh teva*—repeated action becomes second nature," and after a while the *aveirah* becomes mere habit, regardless of whether or not the person intellectually knows the action is wrong. On the flip side—*hergel naaseh teva* in a positive context—when a man repeatedly does a mitzvah, it merely becomes a habit for him to do good things and will ultimately lead to success.

Another indication of this is found when the Torah commands the Jewish people to bring a *Musaf*—an additional offering—on certain days of the year, namely Shabbos, Rosh Chodesh, and the Yamim Tovim. Just prior to listing the *Musaf* offerings, the Torah describes the daily offering that was brought every morning and evening. Since the destruction of the Beis HaMikdash, our sacrifices have been replaced by prayer. The morning and evening offerings are "done" through davening Shacharis in the morning and Minchah in the afternoon.

The *Midrash Tanchuma* on this section reveals an incredible benefit of the daily offerings. The Torah says there will be two lambs brought daily, but then emphasizes that they are not to be brought as one, but rather to be brought separately—one in the morning and the other in the afternoon.

Rabbi Yehuda bar Simone says, "A person will never lie down at night in Yerushalayim while still having a sin in his hand." The Midrash asks, What does this mean? The daily morning offering atoned for the sins a person did the previous evening, while the daily afternoon offering atoned for sins a person committed during the previous day. Therefore, as a person prepared for sleep, he was free of sin because the afternoon offering, the *Tamid shel Bein HaArbayim*, atoned for whatever the person had done that day. The *Tamid shel Shachar* in the morning did the same thing for the nighttime *aveiros*.

Why is it that these *korbanos* ("sacrifices") brought atonement? I would like to suggest that it might have something to do with their consistency. Quite often when a person sins and needs atonement from HaShem, it may take a while for the person to get around to repenting, perhaps even up until Yom Kippur itself. The daily offering is a consistent bombardment of offerings to HaShem on behalf of Am Yisrael; God has, so to speak, no choice but to grant atonement. Think about when a child is relentless in asking parents for candy, eventually it wears them down and they give in. The constant nagging by the child drives the parents over the edge to give in. When God sees us coming every day, three times a day on a consistent basis, He has no "choice."

Coming to shul regularly, doing mitzvos consistently, and davening three times a day will grow and build a person—even if he does not have the best *kavanos* ("intentions"). Whenever a person steadily does something positive, it will become ingrained in him, ultimately guiding him to do what is right and good. The reinforcement from repeating our good actions over and over again leads us to do things better for the right reasons. *Chazal* discuss a person who may do something good but not for the sake of doing what is right, but by doing it over and over again he will come to do it for the right reasons — *mitoch shelo lishmah bah lishmah*.

Incidentally, it is brought down in the laws of *tefillah* that everyone should say the portion of the daily sacrifices as part of their davening. This is the great lesson of the *korban Tamid*. It is a strong message about how we should conduct our lives from the morning until the evening on a daily basis. If we act with consistency, we will install good habits into our daily routines.

◆ ◆ ◆

One of the most inane questions often asked of every little boy and girl is, What do you want to be when you grow up? Typically, the answers range from becoming a doctor, a lawyer, an astronaut, to becoming an animal trainer. Everyone knows that these jobs, like many other jobs, provide some means of support, a way of making a living. There are people who choose a particular career in order to help the world become a better place, whether for people, animals, or the environment. The young child who says, "I would like to be a helping person, so I would like to become a such-and-such so I can help people," is very special indeed.

Life should not revolve around the type of profession chosen in order to make money, but rather focus upon how my particular strengths will best fit with my *middos tovos*—my good character traits. If my strongest character trait is kindness, then I should find work that gives me the opportunity to do kindness for the less fortunate and those in need. If the trait of truth is something that resonates within me, then I should find work that allows me to pursue truth and honesty. The answer to this question of what one wants to become when he or she gets older should be taken from a list of our *middos tovos*. A focus on goodness encourages within each of us ways to nurture our strengths—within any profession—for the good.

Famously, Yaakov wrestles with the *sar shel Eisav*, "the angel of Esav." In *Bereishis* 32:26, the Torah states: "*Va'yar, ki lo yachol lo va'yiga b'chaf yereicho va'teika kaf yerech Yaakov, b'heavko imo*—And when he (the angel) saw that he could not prevail against him, he touched the hollow of his thigh, and the hollow of Yaakov's thigh was strained as he wrestled with him."

The Netziv, Rav Naftali Tzvi Yehuda Berlin, in his commentary *HaEmek Davar* on Chumash writes that the words *b'heavko imo* ("and he wrestled with him") are superfluous. The Gemara in *Chullin* 91 says that up until now the angel was wrestling with him and became ready to let go and leave. Then it was Yaakov who wanted to continue and wrestle with the angel! Since Yaakov retaliated and again wrestled with the angel, he was punished. Why was he punished when it was the angel who started the fight?

The Rabbis explain that the main character trait of Yaakov was love and peace, and therefore, once the angel was ready to leave, Yaakov should not have held him back. Yaakov should have stopped at that point, instead of re-engaging the angel in a fight.

The Ran, Rabbeinu Nissim, in *Nedarim*, makes a very powerful statement regarding a person's behavior. When a person becomes accustomed to doing good deeds, it is as if he accepts upon himself a vow to continue. In Jewish Law, the repetition of doing something three times constitutes a *chazakah*, meaning we have strength to continue in this manner. An individual who continuously makes the right choice, but one time makes a bad choice, is subjected to greater scrutiny and the magnification of his actions. The actions of one demonstrating a certain *middah tovah* ("good character trait") carry the responsibility of always maintaining that level of goodness. The Ran's opinion is that if someone with sterling character deviates from his goodness, even one time acting differently, he is subject to punishment, because this is tantamount to breaking his vow, to violating his *neder*.

The Gemara in *Berachos* 5 relates a similar idea. If a person is accustomed to always going to shul and one time does not show up, then God Himself comes to ask why he was not in shul. Whether or not the person will be punished depends upon whether his absence was due to being preoccupied with a mitzvah. The Gemara points out that this case and treatment applies only to someone who is accustomed to doing the right thing. This idea is highlighted and magnified with rabbis and individuals who appear to be more observant and may be judged differently by their congregants and students. This Gemara addresses the expectations that we tend to form regarding certain people of stature. Usually the members who receive a call about missing services are those who regularly attend. Therefore, being absent stirs a concern as to why they were absent. The person who never shows up does not get the call for missing a particular day!

The Gemara in *Bava Metzia* 84b relates how Rabbi Eliezer ben Rabbi Shimon was severely punished. Why? He always stood to give honor to the Rabbis. One time, however, he did not. HaShem took exception with him, not because he did not stand up for the Rabbis, but rather because this one time he acted differently from his normal good behavior. This is connected to the notion that tzaddikim—righteous individuals—are judged more strictly than their counterparts for the very same sin. Case in point, Moshe Rabbeinu was denied entrance into Eretz Yisrael, while others with far greater sins were permitted to enter.

Therefore, Yaakov Avinu, who was a man who loved peace and sought out tranquillity, was punished because of that one time he became the aggressor. The angel was already leaving and Yaakov would have been left in peace. Instead, Yaakov went on the offensive, and therefore HaShem punished him by having the angel strike him on his hip. Perhaps if Yaakov had not responded in opposition to his natural character traits of love and peace, then we would be permitted to eat real sirloin steak!

The actions of our forefathers are signs for their children. One of the many lessons of Yaakov, albeit a "negative" one, is to never deviate from the good habits that we have formed over the years, to never go contrary to the good *middos tovos* which are within each of us. We each need to identify what each of us wants to become as we grow older. The quest for perfecting one's character is the proper goal of every human being.

Alternatively, it should be noted that a person who has made a habit of engaging in some inappropriate behavior presents the opposite scenario. If one time he goes against the grain and performs the same type of behavior in the appropriate way, then positive reinforcement should be applied. The individual should be rewarded even though it is one good deed among many bad ones. It is not easy to break out of the "bad deed cycle," so let us not underestimate the triumph of the one who does just that!

Going against one's habits is really going against oneself. It can be good—or bad.

Let us ingrain good habits and never stop doing the right things.

IT'S NOT THE LONGITUDE NOR THE ALTITUDE, BUT RATHER YOUR ATTITUDE DETERMINES WHERE YOU ARE HEADED.

CHAPTER THREE
ATTITUDE

Too often in life our mistakes are pointed out, but our efforts to correct those mistakes are not recognized. Even constructive criticism has its limits! Most of us tend to be quick to point out mistakes in others, but we generally fail to recognize and give due praise when the problem is corrected.

Constructive criticism works well when a person is encouraged, in an appropriate way, to work harder or to do more. Unfortunately, without proper follow-up, such as recognizing that the correction has been made, then doubts regarding the sincerity of the original comments are likely to set in. Typically, a person may intend to proffer comments which are meant to be constructive, but may be misconstrued as just plain old criticism. Simply giving a follow-up comment such as "I see you did much better this time" or "you look so much better," goes a step beyond and conveys a deeper level of concern for the person.

There is a parallel situation I sometimes find myself in, whereby the wrong emphasis is placed on a question or a situation. For example, a stranger walks into shul to daven on a Monday morning, a day when congregants will be called up to the Torah. I might ask him, "Are you a *Kohen* or a *Levi*?" Most of the time he responds in the negative, stating he is "just a Yisrael." Perhaps it would be wiser to ask this same question in the positive, "Are you a Yisrael?" With that subtle modification of wording, a more positive yes will be elicited in the majority of cases.

When your children are studying for an upcoming test, focus on giving praise for the correct answers and give encouragement to continue working on the areas that are difficult for them rather than ragging on their mistakes. The heroes and the villains, or the good and the bad guys of our history, guide us as to how to do and not do things in life. The tzaddikim are always looking at the good in every person, situation, and experience, while the wicked do the opposite.

We can see this in the attitudes of Moshe and his first cousin Korach. The Targum Onkelos translates the words *va'yikach Korach* to be "and Korach divided and argued." The word *va'yikach* is usually translated as "he took," but it may also fall under the purview of "rebellion" by taking something that is not yours.

The Apta Rav, in his *sefer Ohev Yisrael* gives a beautiful psychological insight into the personalities of Moshe and Korach. Even a *rasha* who does everything evil still has a piece of good that can be found within him. A tzaddik, as near perfect and righteous as he is, still has a small cell in his body that is somewhat bad. Quoting from Shlomo HaMelech: "*Ki adam ein tzaddik ba'aretz asher yaaseh tov v'lo yecheta.*" Loosely translated, it means: "*There is no man on this earth, even a tzaddik, who does only good and does not sin; even a tzaddik sometimes sins.*" The reverse is true for a *rasha*—a wicked person. There is some good that can be found, even in the wicked. The difference between the tzaddik and the *rasha* is as follows: The small amount of bad found in a tzaddik is considered as a foreign substance within him. So too, the good is in a foreign place when found in the body of the evil person. A truly evil person does not want to have a soft spot in his heart; he would consider that a weakness. On the other hand, a genuinely good person wants to rid himself of every ounce of bad.

We each have a tendency to draw from others, to see the part of another person that resonates within ourselves. When a wicked person speaks to a righteous person, he looks for and draws from the bad which the righteous person has within him. A tzaddik seeks out that little piece of good found within the *rasha* and gives him the benefit of the doubt. Furthermore, once the tzaddik recognizes the good, even in the wicked, he draws it to himself; and, on the flip side, the wicked one who sees bad, even in the righteous, that piece of evil is drawn to him. There is a magnetic pull to each side. The good and evil are more comfortable in familiar surroundings. From this we can understand how there was a complete separation between Moshe and Korach: they had nothing in common.

Perhaps this dichotomy sheds light on the interaction between Moshe and Korach. Moshe always looked for the good in people, hoping to make the most of that goodness to change the person, thereby causing him to become a better human being. Korach, on the other hand, exploited the negative, trying to turn the individual into a completely different person, expanding upon the errors of his ways. As a result of these behaviors, Moshe continued to have patience dealing with Korach because he could sense a sliver of good and tried to change him for the better. Moshe simply could not accept the fact that his first cousin created such a rebellion in Klal Yisrael, and ultimately a rebellion against God. Korach simply attacked Moshe; he worked to expand the negative, trying to expose flaws in Moshe, in order to take him and all who followed him down.

The proof of the profound difference between these two personalities is found in the results. Moshe saved the Jewish people and led them to Eretz Yisrael. Korach took many Jews with him into the abyss.

It all depends on our attitude. Do we look for the good or revel in the bad?

◆　◆　◆

Idiosyncrasies are part and parcel of being human. We Jews are no exception to this rule and also have our fair share of quirks and eccentricities. Some individuals keep their oddities to themselves, while others not only share them, but try to convince others to develop and practice the same behaviors. As I get older (not old!), I have possibly developed a trait of more tolerance. I try to avoid letting certain statements or behaviors rub me the wrong way. Rather, I try to view them as a lack of understanding. After all, we are quick to note the limitations of others, but we each tend to not see our own habits or quirks.

No one is perfect when it comes to doing all the mitzvos of the Torah and following the Rabbinic laws. Nevertheless, all of us choose, consciously or subconsciously, to perform many mitzvos. Within the performance of these mitzvos, some observe the mitzvah with greater concentration, deeper intent, and total commitment, while others do not. However, there is a great variance among individuals and their performance of the different mitzvos. Individuals who may lack steadfastness in some areas actually show great promise in others. Reuven may observe Shimon's apparent lack of correct performance of a specific mitzvah, but Reuven himself may not show much promise regarding another mitzvah which Shimon excels at, exhibiting exceptional *kavanah*.

Each of us has our own approach to *avodas HaShem*—service to God—and our journey to self-improvement. Some may be more intellectual, others may be more hands-on. A handy person is blessed with a talent to do *chesed* ("kindness") for individuals who may not be able to afford a professional handyman. The intellectual, on the other hand, can tutor someone and help him in his learning or he can learn more in the merit of someone. Some approach their *avodah* in a more flamboyant way, needing to do things in front of many people, perhaps the guy or girl who is always in the center circle at a wedding. Others may be more reserved and take a quieter path, perhaps visiting the elderly and the infirm. Each type is precious in his own way. Ultimately, an individual cannot expect to fulfill all the mitzvos all the time and in the best way. That we do as a group—as a people.

It used to bother me when someone complained about how someone else acted, or complained about a certain practice that we do in our community. My immediate gut reaction would be to reprove the person and say, "Well, why don't you do such and such? Why aren't you performing a certain mitzvah which is related to the very thing you are complaining about?" I have come to the realization that people tend to only see the things *they* do as being valuable in relation to what others are not doing. People pick on other's faults, but fail to see their own failings—sometimes in very closely related, similar situations.

Very rare is the person who can step back and strive to understand why the other person may be performing a mitzvah in a certain way that seems to be wrong. Perhaps if each of us takes the time to step back and think about why someone may be doing something wrong, we could come to accept the behavior, and, even more importantly, appreciate the value of each individual and his or her strengths, rather than point a finger. And sometimes we may even come to the conclusion that the other person was actually correct in their approach.

Each and every one of us must be *dan le'kaf zechus*; we must learn to find the merit in defense of the person whom we are judging. In a religious and philosophical manner, we should all become defense attorneys and come up with ways and rationalizations as to why others are doing things "differently." Let's use our minds to defend others, not criticize them.

There are a number of letters in the Torah that are written either larger or smaller than the rest. One is a small *mem* in the word *mokdah*, found in *Vayikra* 6:2, which means "a large fire." Rav Moshe Shternbuch, in his *sefer Taam Va'Daas*, explains that even though the word *mokdah* means "a big fire," it nevertheless has a small letter *mem*. The small *mem* is written as a clear contrast to the implications of a big fire. A large, raging fire can sometimes get out of control, blowing in all directions without maintaining its purpose. It can be very dangerous, causing great damage and harm. The small *mem* is a reminder that the flame of a person should be tempered: The full force of the flame should not be expended all at once. The smaller the flame, the longer the fuel will last and the longer the light will burn.

If a person thinks about his own spirituality and carefully prepares the flame inside of him, then the fire within will last longer. This is indicated in *Vayikra* 6:2: "*Zos Toras ha'olah hee ha'olah al mokdah al haMizbe'ach kal ha'layla ad ha'boker v'eish haMizbe'ach tukad bo—This is the law of the elevation offering: It is the elevation offering that stays on the flame on the Altar all night until the morning, and the fire of the Altar should be kept aflame on it.*" If a person keeps the flame burning on a moderate level, then he won't exhaust all its energy, allowing it to stay lit during the turbulent times when the winds of life are roaring against him. In fact, the Shelah HaKadosh quotes Rav Moshe Cordovero, stating, "It is of particular merit to recite this verse of the fire continuously burning to save oneself from contemplating doing a sin."

One key to growth is moderation and tolerance for ourselves—and others.

Overzealous individuals, who pick and choose areas of others' faults while ignoring their own, are best ignored. We can strive to look away from others' faults and accentuate the positive of their intent, which should ultimately be driven by Halachah, not by philosophy. We should all become more tolerant of others and understand why people choose to do certain things that do not agree with our views or understanding. Keep in mind the flame. Do not abuse it; temper it with patience and understanding, not with judgmental commentary. As *Chazal* teach us, "Do not judge anyone until you are in their shoes" and judge all men favorably.

◆ ◆ ◆

When you judge favorably, you speak differently as well. Let me explain with a story.

I was the proud owner of two birds. For many years, these feathered friends took care of themselves. All I would do is make sure they had food, water, and enough air space for them to spread their wings. About six months ago one of the older birds passed away. Most of the day the house was empty, so it seemed right to maintain two birds in order that they have each other's company. Therefore, I purchased a new young, whitish parakeet named Spunky as a companion for Doe Doe. A few weeks later we noticed this white scaly stuff growing on his feet and beak and the beak became a little disfigured. It turned out that the bird had mites. If this condition was not treated, it could have led to the demise of the bird.

I was able to treat the bird by giving him a warm bath every morning and soothing his feet with Vaseline. Within a few days his feet were back to normal, but during the illness he lost two nails and I was hopeful they would grow back.

The bigger issue was the beak. The mites had gotten onto the beak as well and therefore Spunky had stopped trimming and filing it. (Remarkably, birds and most animals take care of themselves). Since he was not able to file it down, it kept growing like our nails do. Also, the sound of his chirping was altered due to the overgrowth of his beak.

The major problem, however, was that birds use their beaks to climb and swoop up their food, and in combined action with their lower beak, crack open the seeds, grab the food with their tongue, and discard the shells. I now had to wait and see if he could still eat despite his beak being overgrown and out of shape. If he could not eat, then we would have to decide whether to pursue some expensive treatment or not.

I now began to realize the importance of how perfect HaShem makes something and how easy it is to mess it up. We are also blessed with our own type of beaks—our mouths. We are all aware that the Second Temple was destroyed because of *sinas chinam*—unwarranted hatred—among the Jews. *Sinas chinam* is fueled by *lashon hara*—evil speech—and *lashon hara* also causes *sinas chinam*.

Unfortunately, we do not realize that as we speak negatively against our fellow Jew, metaphorically, our beaks start to become deformed. Our mouth starts to lose its original beauty and shape. Rather, we need to constantly trim and refine our lips, guard our tongue, and even clean our teeth in order that only nice things about others are said. If we do not take care of it and work on it, then we forget about how it is even supposed to look and what its function ought to be.

We must remember when we speak what it can do to our mouths and faces. If we speak evil, then the "parasites" affix themselves to our mouths and faces and disfigure them, and it forces us to continually speak evil. Maintaining a spiritually healthy mouth will ensure that only *lashon hatov*—good speech—is formed and not *lashon hara*. By thinking positively of others and speaking positively of others, hopefully our words will be able to build the Temple one brick at a time and we will be able to rejoice in the building of the Third Temple speedily in our day.

◆ ◆ ◆

Life is about building, but some things we destroy instead. It is all up to us. Consider this: There are different methods for accomplishing many goals in life. If a person wants to destroy a building, for example, the method of taking it down is to either explode or implode the building. In life, either of these methods will have a positive or a negative impact on the project. When something explodes, matter shoots out in all different directions and can cause damage to its surroundings. Imploding, on the other hand, usually causes the structure to cave in, sparing the surrounding area from being adversely affected. Within the construction world there are conflicting opinions as to which method is better. Nevertheless, all agree that some damage is inflicted internally and externally, regardless of the method of choice.

When it comes to the challenges which face each of us on a daily basis, we all too frequently tend to ignore or may be unaware of the personal hurt that we may bring upon ourselves and our families. A seemingly unimportant but striking example of this is how people react when attending a sports event and watch a player who does not live up to the viewer's expectations (or his salary). The spectator will often yell inappropriate words to either embarrass or hurt the player. Unfortunately, the spectator does not realize (or even care) that at that same moment he is making a spectacle of himself! The people around him, including his own family, now look at him in a very different light.

In Judaism we find many laws for safeguarding ourselves as well as others.

When a person explodes in rage or anger, he deludes himself into thinking he is only going to hurt the other person. In reality, when a person explodes, he is actually imploding at the very same moment. Chances are good that he is probably hurting himself far more than the other guy. Keep in mind, the hurtful words that are hurled upon another may be forgotten, ignored, and perhaps not even heard by the other person. Yet the individual who hurled the insult has it remaining within himself forever. This creates a profound change in the individual and adversely affects the people around him.

We have all heard of the biblical form of leprosy known as *tzoraas*. The Torah teaches us that *tzoraas* can appear in three different places: one's body, one's clothing, and the walls of one's house. In *Vayikra* 14:35, the Torah states: *"U'va asher lo ha'bayis v'higid la'Kohen laymor, k'nega nir'a li ba'bayis—The one to whom the house belongs shall come and declare to the Kohen, saying: Something like an affliction has appeared to me in the house."* Rashi comments that the word *k'nega* ("something like an affliction") implies that even if the individual is a Torah scholar who knows that it certainly is an affliction, he should not render judgment with a definite statement by saying "an affliction has appeared to me." Rather, he should say "something *like* an affliction has appeared to me." Commentaries explaining Rashi's words state that only the *Kohen* has the authority to make the declaration.

Even if the owner of the house is a Torah scholar and knows the laws of leprosy, or even if the *Kohen* does *not* know the laws of leprosy, it is *only* the *Kohen* who can declare the house either *tamei* ("ritually impure") or *tahor* ("ritually pure").

Rav Reuven Margolios, in *Yalkut Peninim* (his *sefer* on Chumash), focuses (on this *pasuk*) on the word *li*, upon "me." Rav Margolios quotes *Moed Katan* 8, which states that we do not view the afflictions at night, but rather only in the daytime. He also quotes a *mishnah* in *Negaim* 2:3: "In a dark house we don't open the windows to see the affliction."

This common sense etiquette is taught to a *Kohen*: We do not search for the blemishes within the Jewish people as long as they are surrounded by darkness and are hidden. Even if one was to find a blemish of the Jewish people in the dark, it is not necessarily an impurity. If a person does try to look for a blemish in the Jewish people, this is only a reflection of what is seen from the position of the onlooker. If people see the Jewish world in a context of problems, it is usually a reflection on themselves.

If a person speaks negatively about the Jewish people, whether the nation as a whole or about individuals, it not only hurts the person being criticized, it also destroys the person who utters the criticism. When parents speak in front of their children disparagingly about a teacher or principal, or when they speak negatively against the rabbi or disparage the Rebbi, they are destroying themselves and their child. The child hears negative things about a person and he will no longer respect him. The person spewing forth these damaging words also reinforces a lack of gratitude and respect for such worthy individuals.

Thinking that my words will be used to hurt *someone else* ultimately hurts me as well. The hurt to the individual can cause permanent damage which will carry on for generations. In addition, he makes it hard to regain respect from others.

In addition, exploding about others actually leads to imploding one's own family as well. A person may think it's safe to speak ill of others, but in reality he is destroying his own home. Everyone needs to consciously speak respectfully of others and have a positive attitude toward other people. The reward for doing so is quite long-term: you will ultimately build a solid foundation of mutual respect and understanding for yourselves and for your children. This is a foundation which will not implode or explode, but will grow stronger, showering blessings upon others, who, in turn, will shower blessings on you and yours.

◆ ◆ ◆

We read the *Aseres HaDibros*, the Ten Commandments, twice in the Torah: in *Shemos*—in *parashas Yisro*, and in *Devarim*—in *parashas Va'eschanan*. These 10 mitzvos, according to the Shelah HaKadosh, are categories in which all 613 mitzvos can be found. Nevertheless, these 10 stand on their own.

Examining these 10, one wonders, What can come afterward? They seem to include everything. If one could attach an eleventh commandment, a follow-up mitzvah, what would it be? Is there such a thing as an eleventh commandment? The answer is yes!

The political world offered such a concept. While popularized by President Ronald Reagan, The Eleventh Commandment was actually created by then California Republican Party Chairman Gaylord

Parkinson. In his 1990 autobiography *An American Life*, Reagan attributed the rule to Parkinson, explained its origin, and claimed to have followed it, stating, "The personal attacks against me during the primary finally became so heavy that the State Republican Chairman Gaylord Parkinson postulated what he called the Eleventh Commandment: Thou shalt not speak ill of any fellow Republican. It's a rule I followed during that campaign and have ever since."

The Eleventh Commandment sums up a great deal about human interaction. There are individuals with whom you may disagree, argue, and even sometimes dislike. Nevertheless, if someone is on your team, never put that person down. To do so entails putting yourself down in some fashion. This rule (or law) is a fundamental part of all the other laws.

Looking deeper into our Ten Commandments, we can reach further. Our Sages point out: *Aseres HaDibros* begins with the word *Anochi*—I Am—and ends with the word *l'rei'echa*—your neighbor. Herein lies an ethical lesson for all mankind: Try to eradicate the selfishness from within you that is liable to destroy all your good deeds, and cling with all your might to the love of others. Instead of saying "I," say, "your neighbor"! It is the "I" that stands between HaShem and man. As long as man is the slave of his ego, he cannot get close to God.

The *Aseres HaDibros* are divided equally: five commands pertaining to God and man, and five commands pertaining to man and his fellow man. The two pillars of Judaism originate with two verses: in *Devarim* 6:5, "*V'ahavta es HaShem Elokecha—You shall love HaShem your God*," and in *Vayikra* 19:18, "*V'ahavta l'rei'echa kamocha—You shall love your neighbor as yourself*." Possibly this is the so-called Eleventh Commandment. It is the combining of each of the five on both sides that makes it work. The sum is made up of the parts; they are not independent. They are, in fact, dependent upon each other. If we do not recognize our neighbor as someone who is valuable, important, special, unique, and beloved, then we *cannot* identify with the *Anochi*, the "I" representing HaShem.

The Jewish people must come together as a nation, despite all odds and challenges. We, the Jewish people, come from many different cultures, different parts of the world, different socioeconomic backgrounds, and different levels of observance. To God we are all one nation, one people, one family. It is up to us to see ourselves in the same way. HaShem is telling us that He will be our God if we can see each other truly and honestly as our neighbor and brother.

Whether we call it the Eleventh Commandment or something else, we need to pull together in order to make that change happen. I am confident that over the years we will get closer and closer to that unity. Hopefully, this year we will manage to truly "see" our neighbors and to love our neighbors as ourselves, and HaShem will reveal His sense of "*I am HaShem your God*" to us all.

◆ ◆ ◆

One of my favorite sources of information is the highway billboard. Aside from billboards that are inappropriate to look at, a person must be careful not to get fixated on the board for too long, because it is rather important that he should keep his eyes on the road. One of the most dangerous situations occurs when driving with a passenger who suddenly exclaims, "Hey, look at that billboard!" which, of course, you have passed before you could possibly have glanced at it. Even when driving at the legal speed limit (which really does occur once in a while), I find myself turning my head to look at a passing billboard and then, as a last resort, trying to get a better glimpse of it in my rearview mirror. This activity is very distracting, so be extra careful!

Recently, while driving in South Florida, my wife pointed out a few interesting billboards. One of them advertised a surgeon's practice which has performed the most hip replacements in Florida—a state where many senior citizens live. A second billboard advertised a lawyer specializing in "peaceful divorce negotiations." There are, of course, hundreds of catchy phrases and anecdotes to rouse a person's interest in the numerous billboards. One type which I feel is very telling is the advertising of religion. Whether it is medical, legal, or spiritual, help being sold on a billboard reveals a great deal about our society and our lives today.

One of the major principles the world exists upon is supply and demand. Where there is a demand, you can be sure someone or some company will try to supply it. The inverse, of course, is also true: if we did not have that need, the supply would not be necessary. Obviously, it's important to be able to supply those needs when necessary, but can you imagine a world where some of the billboard ads mentioned earlier would not be necessary?

Just think of a world without the elderly falling and breaking their hips, a world where marriages thrive and people remain together, and, of course, a world where everyone knows about God. Unfortunately, this is not the reality of the world in which we live. Nevertheless, we must ask ourselves the question, How can we view these situations in a positive light and eventually remove the need for some of those "negative" billboard signs?

A fascinating disease discussed in the Torah is *tzoraas*—spiritual leprosy. The primary investigator and decider who determines whether or not the color and form seen is in fact *tzoraas* is the *Kohen*. It is interesting to note that in *Vayikra* 13:3, the *pasuk* states: *"V'raah haKohen es ha'nega b'or ha'basar v'sei'ar ba'nega hafach lavan u'maray ha'nega amok me'or besaro nega tzaraas hu, v'raahu haKohen v'timei oso—The Kohen shall look at the affliction on the skin of his flesh: if hair in the affliction has turned white, and the affliction's appearance is deeper than the skin of his flesh, it is a tzaraas—an affliction. The Kohen shall look at it and declare him impure."* The obvious question is, Why are the words which denote that a *Kohen* look at the *nega* repeated?

Two critical reasons are given that really give us deeper insight into our world and into the messages advertised on billboards.

Let's analyze what the *Kohen* sees.

Tzoraas—leprosy—is found, as mentioned earlier, in three different places: a person's skin, his clothing, and the walls of his house. In each scenario, the affected area is relatively small in comparison to the rest; there is more healthy skin, more unaffected material, and more clean walls than not.

The Kutna Rav, Yisrael Eliyahu Yehoshua Trunk, explains that first the *Kohen* examines the area and to consider if it is a *nega tzoraas*. This, of course, brings a lot of negative attention to the person concerned, because we know what sins bring about leprosy (*Arachin* 16a). Despite the small affected area which may or may not become full-blown leprosy, the *Kohen* looks at the rest of the area that is *not* showing any *tzoraas*.

This "second look" gives more balance to what the *Kohen* is trying to determine. It is not just a black and white declaration of the halachic status of the infected area, but rather a sensitive decision concerning a precious Jew.

The second reason offered for the need to look twice belongs to Rav Meir Simcha of Dvinsk, in his master work, the *Meshech Chochmah*. In this work, he says the second checking of the *Kohen* takes into account two other factors that are not dependent on the person's body: time and circumstances. The fallout from declaring a halachic *tzoraas* requires isolation from the Jewish camp. The leper must be quarantined, living away from everyone else. However, the *Kohen* must take into consideration the individual's circumstances. Sometimes there can be a situation where that person needs to remain in the house: thus, tangential reasons that oppose sending him away must be carefully weighed. An illustrative example can be found in one of the first laws of *Hilchos Aveilus*, about mourning. In *Yoreh De'ah* 342, a case is discussed where either the mother of the bride or the father of the groom dies on their children's wedding day. At that moment either the bride or groom becomes a mourner, but the practical *halachah* is that they go through with the wedding and enter the seven days of celebration known as Sheva Berachos, delaying the mourning until a week later. In essence, the Halachah takes into account the time and circumstances of the situation. So it also is with *tzoraas*; it is the *Kohen*'s responsibility to review and perhaps figure out other reasons why the person may be in this predicament, and not just look at the obvious, glaring affliction. The Halachah is inviolate, but we are alerted to the cautious manner and balanced approach that the *Kohen* must pursue. Thus, by *tzoraas*, the "second look" teaches the *Kohen* to prudently weigh the accompanying factors before rendering the decision.

Most advertising and selling of a product is based upon the demand created by society's problems and perceived needs. If society would fix the initial problems and underlying causes for those problems, it could reduce and possibly eliminate the need for people to supply these services. If, for example, everyone ate healthier food and was not overweight, we would not need the plethora of diet plans offering guaranteed success in losing weight. This, of course, is just one example. When it comes to God and religion, focusing on caring for others and encouraging others might decrease the need for outreach.

The message could not be more vital for every one of us. We have a tendency to be drawn to the negative. We market services based on negativity, and we evaluate a person's situation by looking at the negative elements. Taking a second look can get us to strive to remove stumbling blocks in society, in general. And on a specific level, the second look is a call to evaluate individuals in a comprehensive setting. It is our individual and collective responsibility to look beyond and around the obvious. It is part of the old cliche of not viewing the glass as half-empty, but rather as half-full. Let us strive to focus on removing obstacles and promoting the positive.

◆　◆　◆

Do you have a positive attitude? Toward yourself? Toward others? Toward mitzvos? It is a vital question.

Think about it. When a person walks into a shul, he will find many items that are found in all other synagogues, regardless of their stream of identification. There will be a Torah scroll, the Bimah, prayer shawls, a *ner tamid*, and usually, a charity box. Although each of these items is commonly found in synagogues throughout the world, they do not all look or function in the same way.

In many shuls, a person carries the *tzedakah* box around to individuals, encouraging them to deposit their charity. This may be very convenient, but it takes away an element of the mitzvah. In our shul, the *tzedakah* box is big, bulky, and heavy, therefore the mitzvah of giving charity does not come to you; rather you have to go to it. A beautiful scene takes place every morning as people converge in the back of the *beis midrash* in order to *go* and give their daily *tzedakah*.

There are many components of a mitzvah, and a person should keep in mind that the effort involved in performing a mitzvah can sometimes be equal to the mitzvah itself!

The Torah relates how Yosef HaTzaddik performs the preparation for a mitzvah himself and does not relegate it to his servants. In *Bereishis* 46:29, the Torah states: *"Vaye'esor Yosef merkavto va'yaal likras Yisrael aviv Goshnah…—And Yosef harnessed his chariot and went up to meet Yisrael, his father, to Goshen."* This was the chariot that Pharaoh had given to Yosef. Many of the commentaries ask, Did not Yosef have a number of servants who were able to fasten and ready the chariot for him? Rashi explains that Yosef harnessed it himself to show the importance he placed on the mitzvah of honoring his father. He performed the preparations himself prior to setting out to greet his father for the first time in twenty-two years. Yosef prepared for this mitzvah with the same zeal that he performed the mitzvah.

Rav Menachem ben Shlomo, in his work *Midrash Seichel Tov*, expounds upon Yosef's readying of his own chariot due to the great love he had for his father. Ben Shlomo explains that "love and hatred can remove a person from his position of leadership." Love can take precedence over leadership when warranted, as illustrated when Avraham Avinu prepared for the *Akeidah*. The Torah states: *"Va'yashkeim Avraham ba'boker—And Avraham got up early in the morning."* *Chazal* explain that Avraham got up early out of love for his Creator, and saddled his own donkey. In a similar fashion, Yosef harnessed his own chariot. Avraham's love for HaShem and Yosef's love for his father sparked them to set aside their rank of greatness and perform menial tasks normally relegated to their servants. Inversely, hatred also destroys a person's greatness, as elucidated by Pharaoh harnessing his chariot to chase after the Jewish people when they left Egypt. Later on in *Bamidbar*, Bilaam rose early in the morning to saddle up his own donkey. Pharaoh and Bilaam's hatred of the Jewish people spurred them to cast aside their stature and perform menial activities. Their devotion to evil helped lead to their downfall from prominence.

Rabbeinu Bachya gives a third insight into Yosef preparing his own chariot. He quotes *Midrash Tanchuma* 7: "Rabbi Yudan in the name of Rabbi Eivo says, 'Two people in the world, Yisro and Yaakov, saw honor that was greater than had been given to any other creation.' " No other entity ever created—luminaries, stars, or living creatures—had ever been so honored as had Yisro and Yaakov, because they took the initiative to give honor. When Yisro was going to see Moshe, the Torah states in *Shemos* 18:7: "*Va'yeitzei Moshe likras chosno—and Moshe went out to greet Yisro, his father-in-law.*" Was there anybody who saw Moshe go out and they themselves did not go out? The leaders of thousands and the leaders of hundreds went out, and do you think no one else followed them? The Seventy Elders went out, and do you think the others would not follow? Aharon, the *Kohen Gadol*, went out. Immediately, the entire Jewish people went out to greet Yisro, Moshe's father-in-law.

When it came to Yaakov Avinu, it says that whoever saw Yosef harness his own chariot and go up, do you think they did not go up as well? The servants of Pharaoh and the elders of his house went out to greet Yaakov. Do you think no one else went out? Rather, all of Egypt went out to greet Yaakov upon his arrival in Mitzrayim. This concept of everyone going out to greet them fulfills the precept said by Shlomo HaMelech in *Mishlei* (Proverbs) 3:35: "*Kavod chachamim yinchalu—the wise shall inherit honor.*" HaShem says that, in this world, He gives a portion of honor to the elders.

The lesson to participate in a mitzvah is found even when the obligation is someone else's responsibility. How much more so when that mitzvah is ours to do. Running to do a mitzvah is also found regarding Shabbos. The *Shulchan Aruch* tells us that a person should not run or jog on Shabbos, as this is a weekday, nonholy activity. But a person is permitted to run on Shabbos if he is running to do a mitzvah.

Baruch HaShem, in today's times we are fulfilling many of the mitzvos of the Torah. An area that perhaps we can improve upon, however, is in our *approach* to the mitzvos. Whether going over to the *tzedakah* box, filling up the oil for the menorah, picking up our *lulav* and *esrog* ourselves, as opposed to someone else getting it for us, or any other mitzvah that comes our way, let's take the initiative and go to it, instead of waiting for it to come to us. That is the greatest honor that we can show a mitzvah.

I recently heard the following story from one of my Rabbinic colleagues, Rabbi Akiva Males.

> *The other week, while I was waiting in an examing room to see a doctor, I was furiously writing on a pad of paper all the different ideas that were flying around in my head for the derashos and classes I would need to give over during the course of Rosh Hashanah, Shabbos Shuvah, Yom Kippur, Succos, Shabbos, etc. The nurse came in and saw that I was busy with this writing and not looking through their month-old magazines. She commented about how I must be a workaholic or something. I told her that I'm a pretty relaxed guy, but I'm a rabbi, and there is a whole slew of holidays coming up and that I have a lot of work to do for them. Her disposition totally changed as she smiled and gazed out the window and remarked, "Wow. So many holidays one after the next. That must be so beautiful. You're so lucky."*

Jewish life—especially, but not only, the *chagim*—is busy. We all get a little frazzled by its pace. Nevertheless, let's stop and appreciate how Shabbos, Yom Tov, learning, *tefillah*, etc., offer us many opportunities for stepping off of life's quickly moving treadmill. Let's take the time to enjoy family, getting away from technology, and reconnecting with God.

The nurse's attitude was so beautiful and was the furthest thing from the infamous "*shver tzu zein a Yid—it's hard to be a Jew*" mode of thinking that unfortunately can even find its way into our own minds. It is a great reminder of how fortunate we are and how thankful we should be that we are Jews—even busy ones!

Rav Moshe Feinstein, *zt"l*, in his *sefer Derash Moshe*, commenting on *Bereishis* 31:14, states that Rachel and Leah did not consider that the incident of switching places on the night of the wedding was a challenging test. This was the event when Yaakov was supposed to marry Rachel, but Lavan, their father, substituted Leah instead. Rather, it was something easy to do, like all mitzvos. Rav Moshe emphasizes that rather than groan about all the obstacles one has to overcome in order to get by in life as a *shomer Torah u'mitzvos*, one should be on guard to emphasize to one's children that living one's life according to the Torah and mitzvos is really not a challenge at all.

A second reference to this same idea that Rav Moshe has in *Derash Moshe* is found in *Devarim* 30:19, in the words *"u'vacharta ba'chaim— choose life."* There he emphasizes that only joyful mitzvah observance will inspire one's children and students—not mitzvah observance with a *krechtz*. Learning Torah and observing mitzvos must be done with genuine joy. If teachers or parents exude enjoyment in Torah learning and the performance of mitzvos, it will make the greatest impression and have the most influence over their students and children. The challenge is to show that the love of the Torah and its fulfillment is more fulfilling than anything else we have in this world. Rav Moshe wrote these words more than thirty years ago. Not only was it true then, but it is even more meaningful today.

This is but another dimension to the "kids at risk" syndrome. This problem is not unique to today's day and age. This was a problem after the Holocaust and also during other periods in Jewish history. One major difference between then and now is that today we have so many of the comforts of life that really make it *easier* to be a Jew. The problem is making the choice between a religious, observant life or leading a "free" life that is completely unrestricted in every way.

Let us refocus our priorities and recognize the beauty and long-lasting benefits to us and to our families in being a Jew with joy. Not only is it easy to be a Jew, but it's *great* to be a Jew. With this attitude we will be blessed with happy homes.

◆ ◆ ◆

Every so often, we encounter cute signs that are posted in businesses and elsewhere that offer an insightful look at life. One particular quick-witted sign at the barber shop reads in bold letters "Complaint Department" and underneath there is a picture of a hand grenade with a tag attached to the pin that says "Take a Number." Dark humor aside, complaints do not help and, more frequently, they blow up on us.

The Jewish people complained throughout *sefer Bamidbar*. *Chazal*, our Rabbis of blessed memory, teach us that in the merit of Moshe, we received the manna; in the merit of Aharon, we traveled with the protective clouds; and in the merit of Miriam, the Jews had water in the desert. The *be'er Miriam*—Miriam's well—provided water during her lifetime, but dried up after she died. *Bamidbar* 19:1–2 states: *"Miriam died and she was buried... There was no water for the assembly, and they gathered against Moshe and Aharon."* Later, in 20:5, the people complained to Moshe: *"Why did you bring us up from Egypt to bring us to this evil place?—not a place of seed, or fig, or grape, or pomegranate; and there is no water to drink!"*

There is a famous question asked in regard to the examples of food listed that were lacking. In his *sefer Kehillas Yitzchak*, Rav Yitzchak Reitbard of Vilna gives a beautiful parable to explain the troubling words of the complainers, as follows.

A poor person comes to the doors of the wealthy and says, "The hand of God has afflicted me, because I don't have old wine, or a fattened chicken, or milk and honey, and behold I am starving because I don't even have a few morsels of bread!" Wouldn't all those present laugh? If he is really hungry, he would have immediately asked for bread. He would have never bothered mentioning the other items that he doesn't have; those are luxuries! What does he need? He needs basic necessities. So too in our case of the Bnei Yisrael: they complained that they didn't have all of the fruits to eat, yet they didn't even have water! Without water, there can be no life. Water is the only thing that they should have been asking for.

Rav Reitbard explains that there is a vertical line in the text that separates the words *lo* and *mekom* (in 20:5) in order to break up the flow of the verse. This "pause" transforms the meaning of the verse significantly. The verse should not be explained as questioning God: Why did He take us out to this bad place where there are no figs, grapes, pomegranates, and no water to drink?" Rather, the people were first giving a description of this place— no figs, grapes, or pomegranates. This description set a certain tone. Afterward, they then specifically complained that they had no water!

Perhaps the Jewish people actually were going to complain about not having the fruits, but then paused to reconsider and think about what they were saying, indicated by the line which divides the two words? They were about to complain about something (the lack of fruits) but realized that it really wasn't true, just an exaggeration. Instead, they paused and asked only for water, which, in fact, they really *were* lacking.

When people complain, it can be about anything and everything; typically it stems from the reality that they are not happy with their own situation in life. Complaining is an attempt to feel better or even superior. Even complaining about issues that they are not personally involved in can offer a superficial catharsis. However, more often than not, someone who complains usually ends up hurting himself in the process. If you go to the complaint department and you pull the ticket, it will cause that symbolic grenade to blow up in your face. Countless times people grumble and whine about life, their shul, the schools, the community at large—and end up being hurt by their own complaints. Eventually people catch on to the kvetchers and they lose credibility among those who are truly looking to make a serious contribution. Their opinion will be discounted in the future and they will be relegated to the "complainer's booth" — people with whom no one really wants to associate with.

Nothing is perfect in life. Every place or situation surely presents issues, but by simply knocking and nitpicking, the problems will not get fixed. In order to make a situation better, do something positive to bring about a change. Rather than knocking down, nagging, or whining about something as a critical bystander, work together as a community to create positive change.

◆ ◆ ◆

The idiom "living to a ripe old age" is becoming increasingly significant to me. It is not the "old age" aspect that is influencing me, but rather the "ripening" aspect. One is never too young to absorb this concept. Growing old is a process which really does take a lifetime. What exactly is the blessing and meaning of a ripe old age? Why is "ripening" used to express the process of aging?

One of my hobbies is making fruit platters. The art of making a beautiful platter is dependent on the utensils used in preparing the fruit and the fruit itself. If the fruit is overripe, it is too soft and doesn't stand on its own. If the fruit is underripe, the pieces will be hard but not sweet. There is a skill in knowing at what point a fruit is ripe. Unfortunately, most people need to cut open the fruit in order to make that determination. Once it's cut open, however, if it's not ripe, it can't simply be glued back together to continue the ripening process.

As a piece of fruit ripens, the thick, hard skin begins to soften, becoming thinner. The softer and thinner the peel or skin becomes, the sweeter the fruit is.

The process of ripening is similar to the process of aging. When we are young, we tend to have a tough and hard exterior and are not very flexible. Some interpret this as being tough and harsh, perhaps even bitter regarding certain circumstances in life. But as we age there is a tendency to mellow out and become a little softer. Life seems to take on a sweeter taste. Our bodies are similar to the skin of the fruit. We are small and tender when young, slowly developing a thick skin. This protective covering becomes softer as we age. With fruit, the key is to make sure it's eaten before it rots.

Thus, a ripe old age is indicative of a life that has consistently sweetened over the many years. Steadily sweetening your outlook on life, your appreciation of life, your effect on those around you, will counteract and discard the rotting influences and pave the way for a sweet, ripe old age.

◆　◆　◆

We can now go further and derive this beautiful perspective from Torah sources. A famous line in the Torah is: "*R'ei Anochi nosein lifneichem ha'yom berachah u'klalah—Behold, I have placed before you a blessing and a curse."* The traditional or standard approach to this *pasuk* is that we have a choice to be blessed in this world or to be cursed. If we follow the Torah and perform the mitzvos—essentially choosing life—then that is a *berachah* ("a blessing"). If we choose to ignore the teachings of the Torah, then we are essentially choosing death, which is the ultimate curse.

Further on in the Torah, in *Devarim* 16:17, there is another *berachah* of sorts. The verse teaches that every person should give (charity) according to the blessing that HaShem has blessed him with. *"K'virkas HaShem Elokecha asher nasan lecha..."* If HaShem gives a person the wherewithal to give *tzedakah* and the person chooses not to do so, then he will have been living a cursed life. But if a person gives according to the blessings which God has given him, then his giving is a true blessing. His life has been blessed because he knows how to appropriately deal with the blessing he has received.

This *berachah/klalah* ("blessing/curse") vision flows into our personal outlook in life. We have a choice of viewing events and situations for the good or for the bad, to see events as positive or negative, as sweet or bitter. The blessing to us depends on how we interpret and understand something in life. If we merit to view things in the correct perspective, it will be a blessing; if not, it will be a curse. The ability to achieve this requires time, aging, and experience. The tough and harsh side found in youth will be a curse if never properly developed. However, if we are able to change that coarseness and develop a softer, kinder, more caring attitude toward people, then it will be *our* lives that become much sweeter. This accomplishment will be considered the process of sweetening. Our hard peel of youth will be deemed retroactively as sweet—because that is the necessary progression of a sweet life, as well as a fruit. The sweetness of a fruit can only be tasted at the very end of the ripening stage. So too in a human's life, the sweetness can only be determined at the very end of life.

The Torah outlook on the meaning of "living to a ripe old age" is learning the process by which the sweetness of life comes to be. It is *not* just living to an old age. Sadly, just as sometimes a fruit never ripens, so too, there are people who never ripen, remaining hard and difficult throughout their entire lives. These people live a life of bitterness instead of sweetness.

The remarkable aspect of the fruit is that as it ripens, the peel itself becomes more flesh of the fruit, such as a banana or watermelon. The hard peel turns into the meat of the fruit. Our challenge is to transform some of that tough exterior, softening it up and making it part of our internal essence. Deep down, everyone wants to be caring and sweet; it just takes time to convert that change, morphing it into sweetness.

◆ ◆ ◆

There are times in life when we or our children complain about doing things that need to be done...but we do not want to do them. Quite often, the time and energy we expend on not wanting to do something could have been utilized to actually doing that which we did not want to do!

Complaining about something never gets the job done. If our reluctance would be converted into seizing the opportunity to accomplish something, we would enrich our lives immeasurably.

What can we do to ensure that we maximize our time, strength, and efforts? How do we convert our efforts from negative to positive energy?

The Admor Chaim Meir of Viznitz, in his *sefer Imrei Chaim*, proposes an idea and suggests an answer based upon a verse in the Torah. The verse in *Shemos* 8:16 states: *"Va'yomer HaShem el Moshe, hashkeim ba'boker v'hisyatzeiv lifnei Paroh hinei yoztei ha'maymah v'amarta eilav ko amar HaShem shalach ami v'yaavdooni—God said to Moshe, Arise early in the morning and station yourself before Pharaoh—behold, he goes out to the water—and say to him, so said HaShem: Send out My people so they may serve Me."*

The Admor Chaim Meir asks, What is the significance of arising early in the morning?" The most famous reason was that Pharaoh would go out early in the morning to relieve himself without being seen, in order to reinforce the widely held Egyptian belief that he was a god.

A more poignant concept, however, is based upon another verse which is totally unrelated to Egypt, but philosophically appropriate. The *pasuk* in *Bamidbar* 15:20 states: *"The first of your dough should be separated as challah."* This verse is sending a message that when a person arises from his bed in the morning, the very first thing he does is to serve HaShem. As soon as a person wakes up, he should immediately cling and connect to the thinking of Moshe Rabbeinu. This is done by washing hands, saying *Modeh Ani*, and davening. Moshe's pure goal was to represent truth—*emes*—and to fulfill the Torah by turning away from evil and only doing good.

In *Tehillim* 81:7, we find a *remez*—a hint—in the letters of Moshe's name. If you take the first letter of each of the following words, you get a *mem, shin*, and a *hey*, spelling out Moshe in Hebrew: *"Hasirosi mi'seivel shichmo."* Artscroll's explanation of this is that HaShem freed our shoulders from the tasks that a slave performs for a human master, but it is up to us to liberate ourselves from materialistic indulgence and preoccupation (Rabbi S.R. Hirsch). This does not only refer to physical aspects; Moshe was striving to remove the conceptual orientation of doing evil. Furthermore, it is not enough to just cease from doing evil. Another adage which also includes the letters of Moshe's name is *"Secharcha harbei meod—Your reward will be great."* To desist from evil is one step, but the endeavor to permanently remove evil requires that one must *immediately* do good acts; as a result of doing good, the evil will disappear. The gematria (numerical value) of the words *"el Moshe"* is the same (376) as the word *"asu"*—to do. Immediately go do good acts and then evil will not have a place to set in. Good is not the absence of bad, just as light is not the absence of darkness. Rather, good must be done independently of the bad. One must create light and it will then brighten up even the darkness. So, too, if a person does what's right, it will actively push away the bad from approaching.

Moshe needed to be proactive in dealing with the evil king. Even if Pharaoh eased up on some of the bad he was doing, it would not necessarily translate into something positive or good. It takes great wisdom and analysis to realize that we just cannot wait for something good or positive to occur; we have to make it happen by doing it ourselves. As an example, a person may have a bad reputation and try to "fix" it. He'll go around trying to defend or explain why his reputation is unjust, and that he's really a good and caring person. But instead of expending so much energy on lip service, that same time and energy should be spent on building a record of excellent behavior and favorable deeds. Good actions and demonstrations of genuine concern will eventually cancel out the bad reputation. Just do what is right and the bad will fall by the wayside.

People sometimes make lateral moves, failing to make any progress in life. Forward progress takes conscious effort. If we awake each morning with the clear focus of thanking HaShem for our lives and with the conscious intention of doing good, forward progress will take place. We will each make a strong and positive difference. Moshe was all about making a difference in a positive way by not only removing the evil, but more so, by doing the positive.

Let us get up early, say Modeh Ani, and have a positive attitude toward the day ahead—welcoming this day and every day for the rest of our lives.

◆ ◆ ◆

We find cynicism growing in the world; we as Jews need to strengthen our fortitude to withstand this very negative phenomenon. When we encounter a person who grew up in a secular home and subsequently became religious, how do we react? Do we recall his earlier days, doubt his credibility...or do we properly share the joy of such success?

Similarly, a religious person who stumbles and goes off the *derech*— the path. How do we react? Do we somewhat coldly consider this new behavior as indicative of what this person truly is? Or are we focused on arousing in ourselves compassion and concerned enough to daven that he or she will return to the ways of Torah?

The tendency toward harshness and cynicism is quite incompatible with a desire to be compassionate to our fellow Jews. If we feel ourselves leaning the wrong way, we need to redirect our focus to the wisdom found in our Torah and to the true heroes of the Jewish people. Avraham Avinu, in his old age, remarries. Avraham takes a woman whose name is Ketura. Rashi informs us that Ketura is none other than Hagar, and is called Ketura because her behavior and actions were as pleasant as the *ketores* (the sweet smelling incense mixture of a sacrifice). The Kli Yakar comments that the words *"Va'yosef Avraham"* in the beginning of the verse indicate that he took a "second time," that is to say, he remarried Hagar, but now referred to her as Ketura. The Kli Yakar goes on to explain why only now he called her Ketura and not Hagar, as we knew her originally. Moreover, this "positive" name contradicts that which Rashi explained earlier in *Bereishis* 21:14, that after Avraham sent away Yishmael and Hagar, she returned to her father's house of idolatry and worshiped idols once again! So we see that she wasn't as good as we thought she was...or was she?

Rav Shlomo Ephraim Luntschitz explains that Sarah had greater powers of prophecy than Avraham. She saw that Hagar would revert back to idolatry and for that very reason told Avraham to kick her out with her son. During the period of time she lived in the house of Avraham she was good, but then things turned and she went back to her old ways.

At this point in Avraham's life, it would be difficult to understand and justify Avraham taking Hagar back into his life, unless she had done *teshuvah...again*! The only reason he was able to remarry her a second time was because her actions became pleasant and sweet as the *ketores*. Avraham was open to the idea that a person's religious commitment and level of observance can weaken, but are still able to return on an even deeper level. Ultimately, he never gave up on her. Hagar had made a great impression on Avraham, originally coming to his house as a princess of Egypt, the daughter of Pharaoh. Hagar herself declared, "I would rather be a maid-servant in the house of Avraham than a princess in the house of Pharaoh."

All of us need to absorb this lesson from Avraham: no matter how far a person may drift away, not only in overt observance, but also in the deeper commitment of a frum way of life, we should always look forward to his or her return as an observant Jew, and never give up.

On a deeper level, our view of others—and ourselves—should be positive. We all have ups and downs, challenges, successes and failures... but the more positive our attitude is, the happier our lives will be.

KI CHESED CHAFATZTI V'LO ZAVACH—
FOR I DESIRE LOVING-KINDNESS AND
NOT SACRIFICES.

(HOSHEA 6:6)

CHAPTER FOUR
CHESED

ntrospection should be integral to our daily lives. *Chazal* have instructed us to keep a *cheshbon ha'nefesh*—an accounting of our lives—on a daily basis. Before we retire at night, we should review our day, evaluating what was good that should be continued tomorrow and what was not good that should be avoided in the future. This *cheshbon ha'nefesh* exercise is not limited to individuals; it should be made by communities as well.

If a questionnaire were to be sent out addressing *chesed*—kindness— my guess would be that most people feel they perform an adequate amount of *chesed* and charitable deeds. But do we?

In *Bamidbar* (33:1–2), it is written: "*Eileh maasei Bnei Yisrael asher yatzu mei'Eretz Mitzrayim l'tzivosam b'yad Moshe v'Aharon. Vayichtov Moshe es motzaeihem l'maaseihem al pi HaShem v'eileh maaseihem l'motzaeihem*—These are the journeys of the Children of Israel who went forth from the land of Egypt according to their legions under the hand of Moshe and Aharon. Moshe wrote their goings forth according to their journeys at the bidding of HaShem, and these were their journeys according to their going forth."

Rav Yoel Schwartz of Yeshivat Dvar Yerushalayim wrote a beautiful message regarding the travels of the Jewish people. He quotes Rabbeinu Yonah, from his work *Shaarei Teshuvah*, and based upon these verses, he states that it's a positive commandment to contemplate the *chesed* ("kindness") of God. We should remember the entire forty-year journey through the desert. Throughout that entire time God fed us manna, gave us water to drink, our clothing never wore out, and all our needs were taken care of. Today, every member of Israel is obligated to remember the kindness that God does for us on a continual basis.

Rashi comments on this verse: Why were these journeys written? (He answers,) to make known the acts of kindness of the Omnipresent. For although He decreed upon Israel to move them about and to make them wander in the wilderness, they did not wander for the entire forty years with no rest; fourteen of the forty-two places that they wandered occurred during the first year after they left Egypt...which preceded the decree of the wandering itself. In the final analysis, they traveled to twenty-eight places within thirty-eight years.

From this section we learn that there are two areas in which a person is obligated to remember and recount God's kindness to the Jewish people traveling through the *midbar*. The first is that the punishment which was decreed upon that generation was minimized through His kindness. HaShem didn't have to provide us with the comforts and luxuries we experienced during this period of travel that was meant to be a punishment. Yet He did. Second, it is a mitzvah to remember all the difficulties we experienced and to acknowledge the places and events that, thanks to the kindness of God, we endured. The Gemara (*Shabbos* 13b) states that even *tzaros* ("hard times") actually reflect kindness from HaShem. The Gemara relates: "Rabbi Chananya ben Chizkiya wrote *Megillas Taanis* (the Book of Fasts) because they endeared the difficulties in life." The language of *mechavivim es ha'tzaros* ("desiring the hardships and difficulties") teaches us that even when life is hard and difficult we must give thanks to God. The Maharsha comments that the name of the book *Megillas Taanis* speaks of the days we fasted because of the troubles we suffered during our history. Ironically, these days which could have been tragic, ended up becoming festivals, such as Purim. Nevertheless, we still call each of them by the name *taanis*—fast day—in order to preserve the reason that we fasted and the kindness HaShem performed for us.

The Chofetz Chaim wrote in his *sefer Machanei Yisrael* (chapter 39): If HaShem helped a person survive a battle or any other type of difficulty, he must praise and thank God and must be *makir tov*—recognize and remember this act of kindness from HaShem throughout his entire life. The Chovos HaLevavos writes, "A person must recognize HaShem's goodness and thank Him for the ordinary things in life. How much more then must a person thank God and remember a specific or unique kindness or miracle."

Traveling in the desert was dangerous, but we experienced HaShem's protection and He delivered us to Eretz Yisrael. The Jewish people have been traveling now for a few thousand years, and we would not have been able to survive without the *chesed* that HaShem continues to do for us in our journeys through *galus*.

We must constantly thank HaShem for all He has done and continues to do for us. In addition, we all know that the biggest compliment we can give someone is to model our behavior after that person. Perhaps the best way to show our thanks to God and to recognize the *chesed* HaShem has done for us is to emulate HaShem's actions.

Let us commit ourselves to doing more *chesed*. This is particularly relevant when it comes to greeting the traveler or visitor. We must extend a courtesy to that individual. Whenever a visitor enters our shul, we should make them feel welcome by giving them a *shalom aleichem* or another warm greeting, and, if possible, extending an invitation to them to join us and our families for a meal. Isn't this a world that HaShem wants to see?

◆ ◆ ◆

Students and congregants are supposed to learn from their teachers and rabbis. It wouldn't be the end of the world, however, if a rabbi or teacher would take the time to learn something from their students or congregants. Not long ago, there was a news story about a New York City police officer buying a pair of shoes for a homeless man (despite a recent report that the man was not homeless and sold the shoes because he already owned a pair). The act of kindness by the innocent police officer serves as a reminder to us all of the idea of "unconditional giving."

This story was recorded by a law enforcement agent who was visiting New York City from Arizona and it went as follows. "Right when I was about to approach, one of your officers came up behind me. The officer said, 'I have these size 12 boots for you; they are all-weather. Let's put them on and take care of you.' The officer squatted down on the ground and proceeded to put socks and the new boots on this man. The officer expected nothing in return and did not know I was watching. I have been in law enforcement for seventeen years. I was never so impressed in my life. I did not get the officer's name. It is important, I think, for all of us to remember the real reason we are in this line of work. The reminder this New York City officer gave to our profession in his presentation of human kindness has not been lost on me or any of the Arizona law enforcement officials with whom this story has been shared. The officer, who has since been identified as Officer Lawrence DePrimo, has been inundated with support for his act of kindness."

The story was sent to me by a congregant who felt that this kind of inspiring act of *chesed* should be done on a regular basis and that it should be emphasized within our shuls and schools. Unfortunately, the *chesed* and kindness that the *mussar* of the Torah emphasizes is not something we have inculcated enough into our daily lives. Thus, when a kindness or *chesed* is performed, we think it is very out of the ordinary. However, the truth is, it's something we should all be doing. Every human being was created *b'tzelem Elokim*—in the image of God—and therefore should follow in the ways of HaShem. God's existence is all about giving and getting nothing in return. Our lives are filled with opportunities to give unconditional kindness to our fellow man.

When people hear or read about others doing unsolicited kindness, they aspire to do the same. Unfortunately, they often don't. There are two reasons why people hold back:

(1) When the opportunity presents itself, they become shy and hesitate to carry out the kindness. (2) The opportunities are there, but

they are oblivious to them. People often struggle with recognizing and seizing that moment of opportunity.

This past winter I was driving during a heavy downpour. I stopped at a light and noticed a person sitting on the curb without proper protection or an umbrella. I drove right past the person and only later did it dawn on me that I missed a golden opportunity to somehow help that person. I could have given him my umbrella, given him a ride, or even gone a little out of my way and purchased an umbrella for him. I was really bothered by my lack of perception in realizing that this was the opening of a window for me, but I did not "look out."

Recently, though, I was able to stretch out my antennas and tap into the correct frequency of HaShem's message. Twice within the last month while driving, I approached a stalled car in the middle of the road. I immediately pulled over to the side and helped push and steer the car to a nearby parking lot. Interestingly enough, in both cases, other cars sped right by. There were a few others that paused to at least ask if additional help was needed.

I am not writing about these episodes to gloat—each of us is trying to be a little better, one step at a time. We all have failures and successes. We all have the ability to perform these random acts of kindness that will help others in their time of need and make a person feel good about helping. However, sharing these experiences reinforces the notion of *b'tzelem Elokim*—that we are not only fashioned in the image of God, but that we are expected to act that way as well.

In *Vayikra* 19:2, the Torah states: *"Dabeir el kal adas Bnei Yisrael v'amarta aleihem kedoshim tiheyu, ki kadosh Ani HaShem Elokeichem— Speak to the entire assembly of the Children of Israel and say to them, You shall be holy, for holy am I, HaShem, your God."*

The Chasam Sofer quotes Rashi and teaches that this portion was said during *Hakhel*, an entire gathering of the Jewish people—men, women, and children. We see from here that, contrary to popular belief, holiness is not to be attained through separation and solitude, but rather by being together with the people. A person should get involved with people the same way that HaShem does, by doing kindness without expecting anything in return.

Attaining holiness comes to different people in diverse ways. Some feel the holiness through what we call the spiritual side of life: learning, praying, and fulfilling the commandments as they were given. Others climb the ladder of success and want to share what it is like to be a giver for the purpose of giving alone and not getting anything in return. Their ladder of material success is used for *ruchniyus* purposes. When God says to be holy because He is holy, we should do those same acts of holiness, namely the acts of kindness that randomly appear before us. Opportunities swarm around us all the time, but we need to be on the lookout for them. HaShem provides the prospect, but we have to prime ourselves for it.

Being holy is accomplished by walking in the ways of HaShem. God is merciful, just, and compassionate, and He embodies all the attributes, including performing *chesed* for the world. In davening, we refer to HaShem as a *gomel chesed*, one who gives over kindness. This is one of the loftiest attributes to emulate. Next time you see an opportunity to perform a "random" act of kindness, remember that God has sent you the chance to become holy—to emulate the holiness of HaShem.

◆　◆　◆

Doing *chesed* when opportunities arise is crucial. Still, it is reactive. What about being proactive in life?

I recently started playing a board game after a very long hiatus: the game of chess. In the past, I defeated children my age and adults five times my age. Whether or not I truly had this incredible skill to win the game against adults or they were just being nice to a little kid is something I will never know. Either way, I learned to love the game. For those who are unfamiliar with chess, it is a game that makes you think and create strategies in order to force your opponent's king into submission.

We struggle on a daily basis, maneuvering around life's challenges. We try to stay on top of our game, but sometimes succumb to losing something that is either irrelevant or very critical to our survival. We often feel like pawns in a game in which we have no control. We sometimes look at our jobs, work, family, or even purpose in life and feel as though we are getting nowhere. The blame for not getting anywhere or for spinning our wheels can be attributed to our own failings or to sabotaging from others. Unfortunately, these feelings tend to be all too true and are reflected when playing chess. Sometimes the opponent is superior: no matter what I do, I lose. At other times I make poor or wrong moves, and the results are devastating. Whatever the case may be, in chess and in real life situations, we all need to keep focused and concentrate on the King.

While reading about chess, I came across an incredible insight about life. A person of authority was accused of manipulating people and placing them in situations that they considered to be unfair. They felt like pieces on a chess board being moved around from above. The authoritarian responded in a classic way, "I don't move the pieces, I move the board!" L'havdil, HaKadosh Baruch Hu is not actually moving us, but rather He moves the world around us. We then must determine our own destiny by making the correct choices.

There is an eerie similarity between chess and the showdown between Moshe, representing the King of Kings, and Pharaoh. Pharaoh was used as the title given to the king of Egypt. The word "pharaoh," however, originally referred to the palace, later taking on the meaning of "king," the person who occupied the palace. In a series of moves, HaShem outmaneuvers Pharaoh by "checking" him after a series of blows, namely the makkos. In chess, often as a direct result of a difficult or incorrect move, the king will lose one or even more of his pieces (men). So too with Pharaoh. Despite the fact that he manages to wiggle out (by begging for mercy, of course) of the "check," a huge toll is placed upon the Egyptian people, the land, and the economy.

The comparison of kings is highlighted in Shemos 7:15: "Leich el Paro ba'boker, hinei yotzei ha'maymah V'Nitzavta Likraso Al Sfas HaYior, V'Hamateh Asher Nehpach L'Nachash Tikach B'Yadecha—Go to Pharaoh in the morning—behold! He goes out to the water—and you shall stand opposite him at the river's bank, and the staff that was turned into a snake you shall take in your hand."

Rashi explains: HaShem told Moshe to find Pharaoh at the Nile River early in the morning. Since Pharaoh was viewed by his people—and by himself—to be a god, he literally had to sneak to the Nile in the early morning to relieve himself. *Midrash Tanchuma* 14 explains the distinction between HaShem and an ordinary king. An ordinary king needs to attack his enemy by surprise, while HaShem warned Pharaoh time and time again before each and every plague, perhaps in order to offer Pharaoh an opportunity to repent and spare himself and his people from further destruction. The commentary *Eitz Yosef* adds that HaShem sent Moshe to the Nile to catch Pharaoh in his cover-up and to expose his humanity; Pharaoh's physicality exhibits that he is *not* a god. The commentary in the *Midrash Rabbah* 9:8 expounds that Moshe went out to see Pharaoh at the time when his actions displayed that he was not a real Pharaoh.

Midrash Lekach Tov says that HaShem told Moshe to find Pharaoh at the river because Pharaoh kept pushing Moshe away, not allowing him access at the palace. Therefore, Moshe went to the river and literally stood "opposite him" (put him in "check"), cornering him so he could not escape. No other people (or pieces) could interfere or block Moshe from confronting Pharaoh at the Nile. This time Moshe, the messenger of God, the Kings of Kings, was able to "checkmate" the king of mere flesh and blood.

One final observation: In chess, after "checkmate" is announced, the game is simply over. In reality, in order to actually win the game, you need to knock down or remove the king from the board. However, most times the game ends with the call of "checkmate." No one bothers to actually remove the king piece. Interestingly, even after the tenth plague of *makkas bechoros*, Pharaoh was not killed (even though he was a firstborn). He was figuratively left to remain on the board.

The key to success in the game of chess is to always be on the offensive while remaining very cautious in every move. So too, in life, we should not just sit around and wait for things to happen. Instead, we should become the initiators of creating a better life for ourselves and our families. Be proactive in starting a *chesed* group or in organizing a group to learn or to say *Tehillim*. The rule in life should be "get up and start doing things before being asked to do them." Success in our personal religious chess game requires our bringing out the king within each of us and to focus on the King of Kings—*HaKadosh Baruch Hu*. Keeping all this in mind after 120 years on this earth, we will defeat our opponents, physically and spiritually, with a clear, unalterable "checkmate"!

◆　◆　◆

There are people who talk about doing *chesed* and then there are those who actually *do chesed*. Experts tell us that when you need something to get done, ask a busy person, because a really busy person can always find time to do more.

There's an expression, "Oh, he can talk the talk all right, but he can't walk the walk," which basically means that someone talks a good game, but when it comes to action, he is utterly useless or ineffectual. Building upon this, one would suspect that the words "to walk the walk," if correctly quoted, mean "to follow through with real actions on verbal claims or promises."

In *Pirkei Avos* 1:15, Shammai is quoted as saying these same famous words 2,000 years ago: "*Emor me'at v'asei harbei*," loosely translated as "*Say little and do much.*" Rabbeinu Yonah, in his commentary on this *mishnah*, applies this concept to when a person promises his friend to do something on his behalf. This is taught from a passage in the Talmud (*Bava Metzia* 87a), relating a story about Avraham Avinu. In *Bereishis* 18:5, Avraham says to the three angels, "*I will fetch for you a morsel of bread that you may nourish your heart.*" But then in 18:7–8, the Torah gives a detailed description of what Avraham actually did: "*Then Avraham ran to the cattle, took a calf, tender and good, and gave it to the youth who hurried to prepare it. He took cream and milk and the calf which he made and placed these before them…*" Avraham only said a little, but he produced a lot for them. The Talmud contrasts Avraham the tzaddik, a righteous individual, to Ephron the Chitite who was wicked. In *Bereishis* 23:15–16, Avraham comes to bury Sarah, and Ephron says, "*Land worth four hundred silver shekalim; between me and you—what is it? Just bury your dead,"* intimating that Avraham could forget about the money, it was not necessary to pay Ephron. The very next *pasuk* states that Avraham actually did pay the full amount Ephron had demanded, four hundred silver pieces.

It is all too common to find within communities everywhere so many well-intentioned people sitting on school or shul boards and participating in committee meetings, who make grand suggestions about what should or could be done. People enthusiastically come up with wonderful ideas, but they never follow up or make an effort to carry out their own suggestions. The idea may be theirs, but they want someone else to bring it to fruition. Usually out of every one hundred people shouting and barking ideas or orders, only one person actually does the work. The rule in life should be that whoever makes a suggestion should be the one to do it! *Emor me'at v'asei harbei!*

Speaking is great. Doing is greater.

◆   ◆   ◆

Chesed takes on many forms. Consider the following.

Living in San Diego has many benefits, but one negative is the lack of appreciation for the changing of the seasons. Growing up on the East Coast, we looked forward to springtime, when we could really enjoy going outside. Once spring arrived, ball playing and all outdoor activities picked up, leaving winter dormancy behind. As I headed out to take the field or the courts, I forgot how soft and tender my skin had become over the winter. It did not take too long before cuts and scrapes started to show up as I tumbled, rolled, and fell.

I still remember the stinging of hydrogen peroxide as it was poured over open wounds in order to clean out the dirt. It was never sufficient to just put a bandage on top of the cut; it had to be cleaned out in order to avoid infection. Usually cleaning the area in and around the cut and topping it off with iodine was more painful than the cut itself.

As we get older, we recognize that we don't only have physical cuts and bruises; we have emotional ones too. Scars that remain after a physical injury are almost looked upon as trophies of some sort. Physical scars are reminisced and laughed about, even many years later. Emotional scars, however, can't be seen, but are there nevertheless, embedded in our memories forever, sometimes emerging years later.

Often we hear comments, such as, "You shouldn't feel so bad; there are worse cases." Or, "Look at the bright side of things."

Those words may be true and are meant to encourage someone who is down in the dumps, upset, and perhaps borderline depressed. Nevertheless, a person needs to know when it is appropriate to give that type of advice. In my humble opinion, telling someone that his or her situation could be worse should *not* be said when the wound is fresh and open. That kind of remark is only a bandage; it does not solve the problem or address the pain that the person is experiencing now. After the initial wound is cleaned out, only then can we apply a bandage and use that to encourage the healing process needed for rehabilitation. Slapping on a virtual bandage or just telling the person to see the good may all be true, but at best gives poor solace during times of trial or difficulty. These comments, although well-meaning, should come later, after a person has had time to "clean out" the initial hurt.

In a similar vein, in *Pirkei Avos* 4:23, Rabbi Shimon ben Elazar states, "*Al teratzeh es chaveircha bi'shaas kaaso*—Do not appease your fellow in the time of his anger." Rashi explains that this would be an exercise in futility, because he is so enraged at this point. He will remain impervious to conciliatory words until he calms down. Rav Menachem ben Shlomo Meiri, known as the Meiri, says such hasty appeasement comes across as insincere, giving the impression that the speaker has little regard for the recipient's dilemma.

In *parashas Shelach*, Moshe defended the Jewish people and spared them from annihilation. HaShem was furious with us when we wanted to select another leader to take us back to Egypt. Moshe employed a tactic of declaring that the nations of the world would say that "the Jewish God took His people out of Egypt only to kill them off in the desert." Moshe then stated, "*And now, let the name of God become great*" and quoted six of the Thirteen Attributes of Mercy by which God is known (*Bamidbar* 14:1–18). The Netziv gives a very short, but insightful, reason regarding why only a partial listing of the attributes was referred to. Moshe was only looking for those *middos*—those character traits—that would appease HaShem for that moment. The Ramban also mentions the idea that Moshe was not seeking complete forgiveness, but only partial forgiveness, in order to at least get the Jewish people into Eretz Yisrael. Once they arrived there, HaShem would complete the punishment for them and for the future generations.

We understand from the Netziv's explanation that even when it comes to soothing God's anger, we sometimes limit the kind of words we use. These particular six words and phrases are utilized to soften the relationship, confirming the notion of not saying too much. Perhaps if Moshe insisted upon using the full Thirteen Attributes, HaShem would have said, "Moshe, this time the people really went overboard, so do not try to convince Me with those words." Sometimes a person's words can backfire when he's trying to use them to assuage anger or hurt.

When visiting the sick, paying a *shiva* call, or even hearing about a person's *tzarah* ("bad situation"), don't start reciting the cliches of "be strong," "have more faith," "it could have been worse," etc. Only after the individual has fully digested his or her new situation is it time to strengthen him with words of *Chazal*.

Throughout the course of my career, I have come to understand that it is so much easier to state words of comfort and to speak in clichés of the Rabbis than it is to be on the receiving end: to listen passively and politely. During the initial period of hurt, regardless of the nature or severity, all a person should do to help is to listen to the person kvetch it out. Let the person spill out his guts and feelings of how difficult, challenging, and perhaps even overwhelming life is. Even if he says "life isn't fair," you should respond with compassion and understanding.

Sometimes, listening is the greatest *chesed* of all.

◆　◆　◆

Sometimes, *chesed* is even harder. Sometimes, *chesed* involves forgiveness.

Often in life, we do something wrong to another person. As we regret our actions, we typically will approach the person and apologize. The Rabbis teach us not to be cruel, and therefore, to forgive when asked. In many people's minds the thought of "maybe they didn't really forgive me" lingers. A person always knows his own level of sincerity, but how does he determine the level of sincerity from the forgiver?

At a certain point, we say to ourselves, "I have done what is required of me. I know I was sincere when I apologized, and if the other person really does not forgive me, so be it. It's his problem now!"

It is out of our hands as to whether the victim will forgive us (the sinner) if we sincerely ask for it. A more difficult assessment is if we are the victim, and with all sincerity forgive the sinner, yet the sinner may not be convinced that we truly did forgive him or her. What can we do to convince the wrongdoer that it's okay; let's move on and forget about it?

Everyone has a different understanding and explanation of what makes someone a tzaddik or *tzadekes*—a righteous man or woman. Every person, when asked to define "a righteous person," will describe a different trait in which that individual may excel. The person will go above and beyond the average person in a certain area of life. Sometimes a person cannot describe what a tzaddik or *tzadekes* is, but when they see one, will say, "Now *that* person is a righteous individual." When you see a righteous person, you recognize the inner beauty of that individual; you know this person is a tzaddik or a *tzadekes*.

Yosef is referred to as Yosef HaTzaddik. We can look at Yosef's life and pick out many reasons why he earned such a title. I believe there are some more obvious reasons why he is called a tzaddik, but then there are some less obvious ones as well.

The Kli Yakar reviews a behavior of Yosef that is perhaps less obvious to us regarding our definition of "righteous," but nevertheless it is an act of deep significance and attests to his greatness. When Yosef revealed himself to his brothers, they were in such total shock and disbelief that they could not speak. Yosef did not wait for them to respond, but rather continued with a lengthy discourse about how "HaShem has a master plan and I am supposed to be here in order to sustain the family." Yosef, in this manner, is telling his brothers that he forgives them, because, in reality, it was necessary for things to end up this way. Nevertheless, the brothers never felt comfortable with the idea that Yosef really forgave them. Perhaps Yosef was only extending himself to his brothers as long as their father Yaakov was alive.

When Yaakov died, once again this inner fear returned to the brothers; they were afraid Yosef would take revenge. The brothers threw themselves onto the floor and bowed before Yosef and declared, "Behold, we are your slaves." Yosef answered back by telling them that only HaShem is the Master. "You thought badly of me, but rather HaShem has looked well upon us to thrive as a great nation." Finally, as Yosef still saw disbelief in their eyes, he told them (*Bereishis* 50:21): "*And now do not be afraid, for I will provide for you and your children.*" Here, the Kli Yakar explains that Yosef was trying to convince his brothers once and for all that he had forgiven them. He explains that Yosef sustained the brothers when there was plenty of grain stored up in Egypt and he was busy providing for the Egyptians. Now the famine had returned even harsher than before, and perhaps one could argue that Yosef would not give them food because he didn't have enough for everyone. Therefore Yosef told them, "I will sustain you at whatever price I need to pay." Be it socially, economically, or politically, Yosef was guaranteeing the safety and security of his family—the ultimate sacrifice on Yosef's part. This unequivocally demonstrated that Yosef really forgave his brothers—not only at this point, but from the very beginning.

The lesson learned from Yosef HaTzaddik in regard to forgiveness is to keep on forgiving. If one feels any doubt as to whether or not the victim truly forgives, then the victim (as in Yosef's case) must find every opportunity to reassure the sinners that they are forgiven. This is true forgiveness; Yosef repeatedly tells his brothers that their actions were part of God's plan. This is an aspect of *tzidkus* ("righteousness") that Yosef displayed, and that is why he was Yosef HaTzaddik!

◆ ◆ ◆

Sometimes, *chesed* is quite easy.

In each and every generation, new forms of communication are established. One of the most basic kinds of communication is a greeting. Greetings and salutations set the tempo and tone of our interactions with each other. These greetings, whether a simple bowing of the head, a symbolic kiss on the hand, or even just a wave of acknowledgment, reflect the differences in cultures. All, however, indicate that some type of interaction is about to take place. Here in America, greetings have evolved over time from a firm handshake to what we now call a fist bump.[1] When I was a kid, we used to give a high-five. Then a low-five was in style. What is the sublime message of these different forms of greetings?

A handshake is one of the strongest greetings we have. A handshake involves an outstretching of hands to each other and a grasping of the other person. When people shake hands, there is a touch and feel of the other person. In truth, there are a variety of grips that people have when they shake—some firm and some feeble. There is a shake where a person even puts his second hand over the other person's hand, and then there is the yeshivishe shake with just the fingertips. More significant with regards to the handshake is that the people can look

---

1 The fist bump (also called Fo' Knucks or knuckle bump) is a gesture similar in meaning to a handshake or high-five. A fist bump can also be a symbol of giving respect. It can be followed by various other hand and body gestures, and may be part of a dap greeting. It is commonly used in baseball as a form of celebration with teammates and with opposition players at the end of a game.

The gesture is performed when two participants each form a closed fist with one hand and then lightly tap the front of their fists together. The participants' fists may be either vertically-oriented (perpendicular to the ground) or horizontally-oriented. Unlike the standard handshake, which is typically performed only with each participant's right hand, a fist bump may be performed with participants using either hand.

According to *St. Louis Post-Dispatch* columnist Bernie Miklasz, the fist bump was created by Hall of Famer Stan Musial as a way to prevent catching colds from shaking so many hands. *Time* magazine wonders if it evolved from the handshake and the high-five. They cite knuckle bumping in the 1970s with NBA player Baltimore Bullets guard Fred Carter. Others claim the Wonder Twins, minor characters in the 1970s Hanna-Barbera superhero cartoon "Super Friends," who touched knuckles and cried "Wonder Twin powers, activate!" were the originators. However, the fist bump or pound can easily be traced as far back as the late 1800s and early 1900s to how boxers greeted each other in the ring while they were wearing their gloves. In fact, the fist bump's origins may well lie in the animal kingdom, as the gesture is natural behavior observed in primates, according to a book published by Margaret Power in 1991.

at each other, make eye contact, and affirm that which is taking place through their hands.

The greeting in the Orient of bowing is very hands-off; there is no bodily contact and, to the Western viewer, can be seen as somewhat cold. The Sephardic custom (and the Arab custom as well) is one of the oldest forms of greeting: a kiss on both cheeks. This kissing is, of course, only for the men, as there is no kissing publicly between men and women. We find the greeting of kissing in *parashas Va'yishlach* 33:4, when Yaakov met up with Eisav for the first time since Yaakov had fled from his home. The verse describes that upon meeting, Eisav kissed Yaakov on the neck. There are dots written in the Torah over each letter of the word *va'yishakeihu*—and he kissed him. Rashi and many other commentators explain the dots to mean an insincere kiss. In fact, some say Eisav tried to bite Yaakov on the neck (like a vampire) to kill him. The *Sifsei Chachamim* explains the missing dot over the Hebrew letter *shin*—that leaving it out spells *va'yakeihu*, which means "to knock out." Similarly, in the Haggadah of Pesach, where it says, *"hakhei es shinav"* regarding the *rasha*, we see that the word *hakhei* refers to the losing of teeth. In our context, Eisav breaks and loses his teeth trying to bite Yaakov's neck. Kissing on the neck, therefore, can be used in a deadly fashion, thus, the gesture of the act can go either way. A person cannot discern whether the intention of the kiss on the neck is a greeting or an attack.

Although the fist bump may be in fashion, pushing and punching away from the other individual leaves much to be desired. Compared to a handshake, we do not find a fist bump to have any great purpose. Halachically speaking, a handshake has significance regarding acquisitions. One of the many forms of *kinyan*—acquisition—is a formal handshake. It is also proper etiquette to remove one's glove before shaking hands. I don't intend to ban the fist bump altogether, nevertheless, let's retain and maintain certain gestures that are part of our eternal society. Let us use a handshake when it is required and not replace it with a new fad. Maintaining the fiber of our society is extremely important and we must safeguard it from deteriorating. Our feelings of communication should not appear to have dots all around, introducing the possibility of insincerity. Rather, we should be clear when expressing our feelings with a warm, firm wrapping of our hands together.

LIFE IS NOT ABOUT HOW MUCH
MONEY ONE HAS, BUT WHAT
ONE DOES WITH IT.

CHAPTER FIVE

MONEY

There are many sayings that are not just cute—they are actually very true! "Bulls make money, bears make money, and pigs get slaughtered." Investors make money in a bull market when the stock market is up and running high, but the investor will choose to sell before the stock goes even higher, having taken a profit already. A bear market is when the stocks go into hibernation, yet investors can make money selling short, betting on the stocks as they drop. Once again the investors must take their gain off the table before it is too late. The pig tries to gain and profit to the very last penny and often loses everything; he gets slaughtered. It is a pretty simple saying that conveys more than the first glance reveals. Its meaning is as follows: do not let greed affect your judgment. While this seems simple, its applications are many.

The stock market and other investments can punish greed when the investor has unreasonable expectations. An investor who is doing well might expect to do even better in the future, ignoring "reversion to the mean," commonly causing the investor to hold onto stocks past the optimal time to sell or overpay for new holdings. This mistake commonly occurs in bubbles. I am only too familiar with this syndrome.

In fact, very often, greed kills. It can kill investors' returns by making them act in haste. The best investor is the one who is intellectually flexible and dispassionate in analysis. As Warren Buffet said, the critical determinant in an investor's success is not intelligence or skill, but temperament.

This concept is not new to the Jewish people. We know it by the saying: *"Tafasta merubah lo tafasta, tafasta me'uta tafasta."* Loosely translated, it means: "If you grab onto too much, you will not grab anything; if you grab a little, then you will seize it." These words are found no less than seven times in the Babylonian Talmud and once in the Talmud Yerushalmi. Rashi, in *Chagigah* 17a, explains the benefit to this precept. Rashi states: "Every place where you find two paths or ways, one approach seizes a lot and the other seizes a little. It is better to snatch the smaller one, because even if you deserved the larger one, but grabbed the smaller one, at least you grabbed something. For in the big one contains the smaller one, so you got at least a piece of the larger one. But if you grabbed the larger one, but were only entitled to the smaller one, then you are trying to take that which is not yours."

It is important to remember that HaShem decides on Rosh Hashanah how much we are to receive in the course of the year. It is possible for us to fritter away the money and opportunity that God was actually giving us; therefore we should take it when it is offered, and if it falls short of what we are supposed to get, HaShem will arrange for the remainder to reach us in another way.

We find a similar lesson in *Bereishis* 33:9–11. The Torah states: *"Eisav said, I have plenty, my brother; let what you have remain yours."* But Yaakov said: *"Please do not! If I have now found favor in your eyes, then accept my tribute from me, inasmuch as I have seen in your face, which is like seeing the face of a Divine being, and you have been appeased by me. Please accept my homage which was brought to you, inasmuch as God has been gracious to me inasmuch as I have everything."* He urged him and Eisav accepted.

Rabbi Avraham Shmuel Binyamin Sofer, in his work *Ksav Sofer*, quotes an idea from his father, the Chasam Sofer. A wicked person, a *rasha*, is never satisfied and never gets his fill. Therefore, Eisav said the words *"yeish li rav*—I have plenty"…but not everything. Yaakov Avinu, on the other hand, uses the words *"yeish li kol*—I have all I need," because a tzaddik, a righteous person, is satisfied and feels satisfied with that which HaShem gives him. This is accentuated by the end of his words: *"ki chanani Elokim*—God has been gracious to me," and therefore I am satisfied with my lot.

The Ksav Sofer adds his own words of understanding to this concept. Wealth and gifts that come to a person through *mazal* are never sufficient. The nature of mankind is to seek out more. Shlomo HaMelech said that someone who loves money will never be satiated from money. But wealth that comes from HaShem comes with an added benefit. That added benefit is *histapkus*, which means "satisfaction, gratification, and contentment." The true *berachah* of wealth is not just having the physical item; it is also being content with it. This is the *berachah* that Yaakov received from HaShem—the blessing of feeling satisfied. Once we are satisfied with what we have, we need not seek out more.

Yaakov tried to reach out to his brother and give him the gift that keeps on giving—*histapkus*—the blessing of learning to be satisfied. Once a person is able to control his thoughts and feel contentment, then he will not have the urge to seek out more, nor bear the pain of not having more. Therefore, Yaakov begs Eisav to take his offering so that he will enjoy all of his possessions with satisfaction. Eisav's statement of *"rav*—(I have) plenty" reveals his true feelings that he is neither content nor satisfied with what he has. Yaakov recognizes this problem within his brother and therefore adds the words *"chanani Elokim."* This is an extra special added bonus which purifies all that we receive from HaShem.

This attitude is not an easy one to learn and accept, but it will make life far more pleasant and gratifying. Take a small gain. Do not risk losing it all by holding on and not selling, hoping for more and more. Take your gains and HaShem will bless them for you to enjoy. *Histapkus*, the blessing of understanding restraint and of being satisfied, is an important key to living life with the fullness of genuine contentment.

◆ ◆ ◆

Are our lives today busier and more frenetic than the lives of our immediate ancestors and even the lives of our forefathers? In today's day and age, life is so much more complex than it used to be. An example is travel. Today, when preparing to go somewhere by plane, we must take into account the money it costs, the time which will be invested, the weather and possibility of delays, and the risks that are involved. Traveling by car is wonderful if it works; but if the car breaks down, then there are a series of woes that come with it, not to mention the extra time and expense incurred.

We live at a time filled with many modern conveniences which can sometimes stifle us, particularly when they break down. We have become so dependent on our cell and smart phones that we panic when the system goes down, when our texting doesn't work, or when a battery needs to be replaced. When the washing machine goes on the fritz, we go insane as to how to deal with the laundry, yet only a few generations ago people wore their clothing for longer stretches of time before washing them. A broken freezer or refrigerator can create an emergency situation requiring a community of people offering to store food which would otherwise be in danger of spoiling.

One might reply, "Sure we have glitches with our modern-day technology, but the advantages far outweigh the disadvantages and inconveniences, *even* when things break down." That is all very true, but Hillel teaches us in *Pirkei Avos*, Ethics of our Fathers 2:8: "*Marbeh nechasim, marbeh daagah*—The increase of possessions and material gain brings along an increase in anxiety and worry."

The ability to travel is wonderful, but is also considered to be *marbeh nechasim*—increased possessions—and it runs the risk of excessive anxiety. Thus, the past generations endured the same level of uneasiness and concern when they had more in terms of the lifestyle of *those* times. Travel was certainly far more dangerous and risky, and there were no cell phones available to call for help. Every generation experienced their "technology" and their accompanying frustrations; all of us must deal with the fact that things do not always work out as planned. What is the proper *derech* ("manner") and Torah outlook or philosophy in dealing with situations that frustrate us and drive us just a little bit mad?

The answer to this is found in the Torah. In *Devarim* 8:11–14, the Torah states: *"Heeshamer lecha pen tishkach es HaShem Elokecha... pen tochal v'savata... v'ram l'vavecha v'shachachta es HaShem Elokecha—Take care lest you forget HaShem, your God...lest you eat and be satisfied...and your heart will become haughty, and you will forget HaShem your God..."* The Netziv, Rav Naftali Tzvi Yehuda Berlin, in his work *HaEmek Davar*, explains that there are two places in which the forgetting of God is mentioned. Earlier in *Devarim* 6:12, the warning of forgetting HaShem takes place at the time when the Jewish people were conquering the land, reminding and warning them—and us—that victory and success should not serve as a distraction from HaShem. Here the Jews were already settling the land and building their homes and dwelling in them. The second instance is a general warning about remembering HaShem even in the *galus* ("exile").

The two warnings of forgetting HaShem come about in different ways. When the people were fighting and conquering the land, they were told to remember HaShem so that He would help them win the battles. Later, when the Jewish people were benefiting from the fruits of the land and becoming wealthy, they were again warned not to forget about HaShem. A Jew needs to reject the natural thought that it was his own strength and wisdom which brought about all of his wealth and plenty. *Berachos* 32 states: *"A full belly is one of the bad sins a person can have."* It can lead a person to forget about God.

The *Mincha Belula* uses the need for bloodletting as an analogy to amassing wealth. He explains that increasing in wealth for its own sake damages both the body and the soul. Money gained with no thought to giving and sharing is sinful. We are required to give. To gain in wealth without sharing it with those in need, with our schools and shuls, is harmful—spiritually and physically. We are taught that we must shed a portion of our financial gain by giving some of it away—by giving *tzedakah*. The reward is both immediate and great: it is a healing for our souls.

As an interesting aside, current research supports the view that those who give generously of themselves and their wealth live happier, healthier, and more fulfilling lives. A person who has earned or inherited wealth will not necessarily sin unless he forgets about HaShem. Having a lot of money is not intrinsically evil; we just need to remember where it came from and where it has to go. Giving—sharing our wealth—is analogous to giving a portion of ourselves. As a person works to amass wealth, he should always remember HaShem, and he should always thank HaShem for his success. Once success has been attained, it is mandatory not to become complacent, and to always remember from whence that success has come. When we forget about HaShem, when we think that we are in control, things have a tendency to spin out of our control. The wealthy person can either shed a portion of his money by giving *tzedakah*, or HaShem will cause the money to be wasted away on worthless items or taken away by some other means.

The modern conveniences, comforts, and pleasures that we enjoy each day are, in essence, a form of the wealth that we amass over the course of our lifetimes. We normally do not forget HaShem while we are working to improve our lot; thus, we should not forget HaShem once we have attained our goals. When challenging situations arise, we should strive to take them as a personal lesson; each one of them is a sign from HaShem that we are not thinking about Him enough. HaShem creates these challenging situations to make us refocus on God and all the blessings that He has bestowed upon us. This, alone, is a profound blessing.

Pay close attention to those seemingly large challenges which, in the grand scheme of things, are really very small. It is not the challenge that we should focus on, but rather the attention HaShem is giving us to get closer to Him. Therefore, the challenge itself, as large and difficult as it may seem in a physical manner, points to a far greater spiritual quest to attain a stronger relationship with HaShem through His intervention with us.

◆ ◆ ◆

Whether it's our body, our possessions, or our money, we may tend to subscribe to the notion that we own it and it's ours to do with as we please, but this is essentially a non-Jewish belief. We believe everything belongs to HaShem and we are the custodians of the material things that God gives us to steward in this world. The notion that everything belongs to the individual is a sign of *gaavah*—haughtiness. The humble individual understands that everything which God blessed him with serves only to test him to see if he will do "right" with his endowments. This is by far one of man's greatest challenges in his service to HaShem and mankind.

Too often in life, we find great people rise and fall due to their inability to handle the blessings of wealth that God gave them. Rather than being satisfied and realizing their responsibility to use their money in a good way, they use it as a weapon to hold worthy institutions hostage. There is no clearer example of this than Korach, Moshe's cousin. Korach used his money and wealth to impress others, and he used it as a means to challenge Moshe. But there was another side to Korach. Not only was Korach wealthy, but according to *Midrash Rabbah* 18:3, Korach was a great *talmid chacham* and one of the bearers of the *Aron HaKodesh*. The *Zohar* 3:49 describes Korach as the *Levi* ("Levite") with the greatest potential.

If so, what happened? What made Korach so rich and how did he lose it all?

In *Bamidbar Rabbah* 18:15, the Midrash relates that Korach was the overseer of Pharaoh's house, and the keys to Pharaoh's treasuries were in his hands. *Pesachim* 119a states: "*The keys to Pharaoh's treasury were a load for three hundred white mules.*" The Gemara continues by stating: "*The Holy One, Blessed is He, said to Korach, 'What benefit do you have from this? You will not have control over the treasures. They are destined for Israel, who will be sent out of Egypt. But as for Korach, he shall not be rich nor shall his substance continue. After he dies, even his own personal wealth will not go to his children, for it will be devoured by the earth.'*" A second explanation, which the Maharsha gives, is that Korach discovered a treasure that Yosef had accumulated through selling grain during the famine and had hidden.

The Rashbam in *Pesachim* 119a offers an insight into why Korach lost everything. He quotes from *Koheles* 5:12: "*Yesh ra'a cholah raeesi tachas ha'shemesh, osher shamur livalav l'raaso—There is a sickening evil which I have seen under the sun: riches hoarded by their owner to his misfortune.*" This refers to the wealth of Korach; as a result of his great wealth, he became haughty and was removed from this world. Unfortunately, people don't realize that even if a person works hard to make his money, it is still only because HaShem wants him to receive it. Many smart people work hard and do not make a lot of money. It is not up to us—it is up to Him.

Chazal, the Rabbis of blessed memory, tell us that a shul is a *mikdash me'at*, a small sanctuary representing the Beis HaMikdash. There are entire tractates in the Talmud and dozens of chapters in the *Shulchan Aruch* dedicated to the holiness of money that is associated with shuls, schools, yeshivahs, and *kollelim*. If two people are in a monetary dispute, there is an avenue of Beis Din to hear their claims. What would a person do if he had a dispute with an institution that represents HaShem? Even if there is a doubt as to whether the individual may be in the right, is he still going to risk being in the wrong? How will a person answer to God after 120 years when questioned whether or not he owes the money?

Sadly, this dispute can spill over into the personal relationship that an individual has with an institution. Frequently, such a dispute can take on the signs of a *machlokes* ("strife"), which will eventually come to no good. By rearranging the Hebrew letters of the word *machlokes* to spell *meis-chaluk*, this strife translates as a division so severe, that it causes death. Since the Jewish people are sometimes viewed as a single individual, a disagreement which becomes severe can cause a separation or parting of the body, making continued existence impossible. We are each required to recognize our place in the world and the unique role each one of us is expected to play. We are also required to recognize the worth and the contributions of our fellow man.

By creating division, Korach actually killed himself and his family; his arrogance led directly to the earth swallowing him, his family, and all his wealth.

The Arizal teaches that even a great person can fail and falter in a *machlokes*. He points to the words in *Tehillim* 92: "*Tzaddik ka'tamar yifrach—the righteous, like a date, will sprout forth.*" The final letters of each word spell out "Korach." A person who does not keep his word or who chooses to use his money or his influence for ulterior gain or to create an environment of contentiousness can negatively affect the community as a whole, actually causing the infrastructure of the Jewish people to tear apart. In the end, such a person will ultimately find himself cast down. The righteous and those who are in a position to support learning are more susceptible to follow in the footsteps (Heaven forbid) of Korach.

There is a certain *siyata di'Shemaya* ("Heavenly assistance") that is granted to Jewish institutions and to their leaders. People should think very carefully before promoting dissension with Torah institutions. To do so is an affront akin to arguing with the treasurer of the Beis HaMikdash, and, ultimately, with the true owner of the funds— the Almighty. Take great care when dealing with money for Torah institutions. This is *mamon hekdesh*—holy money. Give the shul, schools, and any Torah institution, the benefit of the doubt. It is incumbent upon each of us to work together to build up our community.

Korach was haughty; he used his wealth for self-gratification, ultimately destroying himself and his family. May we learn from this to flee from all strife that is not for the sake of Heaven. Instead, let us work together to build *shalom*—peace—and unity in the service of HaShem.

◆ ◆ ◆

During the past decade there has been a see-saw effect in action in the world's economy. (Objectively speaking, this economic cycle affects the world on a continuous basis.) One of the main reasons the economy was hit hard during the last go-around was due to the credit crunch. In simple terms, Americans were borrowing much more than they could ever pay back, which resulted in a lending freeze and an overall tightening of the credit system, vital for a society to grow its economy.

In my humble opinion, as one who was also overextended, it was a good idea to tighten up credit limits and encourage people to learn to live within their means. It can definitely be an inconvenience at times to not have a credit line available, but in the end, a little pain or restraint now results in a lot of gain later. An important lesson here is that it is good to have credit available, but bad if you use it and cannot pay it back. Ironically, having too much credit and *not using it* can also be detrimental to your overall credit and financial picture. At the end of the day, a robust amount of credit may not be so bad in the physical world...but in the spiritual world, having too much does not necessarily translate into good. It can be detrimental.

The Torah states in *Shemos* 36:5–6 that the Bnei Yisrael were bringing more than enough (jewelry, skins, wool, and linen) than was needed for the building of the Mishkan, and so they were told to stop. The second Gerrer Rebbe, known by his work *Sfas Emes*, tries to explain this lengthy discussion regarding the surplus of funds that was collected, and reveals a critical consideration and warning when it comes to serving HaShem. He states that a person wanting to serve God may be influenced and tainted by a personal agenda unbeknown to that individual.

One must keep in mind the building of the Mishkan and all of its components. Every aspect of the construction needed to be on a consistently holy and pure level, without a trace of damaging thoughts. When the Sages and righteous leaders beheld the influx and overwhelming outpouring of generosity, they became concerned. They suspected smidgens of false intentions that were not for the sake of God, but rather for ulterior motives.

It is said in the name of the Baal Shem Tov that a person must see to it that all of his efforts in his service of HaShem are tinged with fear and *bushah*—shame. Often a person becomes haughty after finishing a job or a big project, taking credit for all that he did. To avoid such a situation, a person must "look behind him" — consider Who was there behind the accomplishment —and think about before Whom he standing and for Whom he is working. Stop in the middle of work and remind yourself that you are standing in front of HaShem. When one stops and contemplates who he is truly working for and who he is serving, he will consistently adjust his own actions and refine his mindset. This, in essence, is what the Torah means when stating, "And the people were restrained from giving." They immediately stopped giving too much, and instead stopped and thought about why and to Whom and for what reason they were donating to the Mishkan. Their efforts were exclusively for the sake of building the Mishkan; they were not giving in order to show off to others how much they gave!

We all recognize that the maxim *"Da lifnei mi ata omaid*—know before Whom you stand" refers, in general, to prayer. However, this advice goes beyond the spiritual plane of davening in a shul and associates it with mundane activities, such as donating charity for worthy causes. No matter how much a person gives to charity, he must be careful, continuously reminding himself of this precept.

The Chidushei HaRim, the first Gerrer Rebbe, explains the *pasuk* in *Shir HaShirim* 7:2 as follows: *"Your footsteps were so lovely when shod in shoes, O daughter of nobles…"*—the word for "nobles—*nediv"*—can also be read as a *nedavah* ("a pledge"). A person's pledges and donations also need the protection of a "shoe" so that the intentions and purpose of the donations do not go astray. With this we can come to understand the first *mishnah* in *Shekalim* 1:1: "On the first of Adar, the Beis Din proclaims regarding the payment of the shekalim (half shekel everyone donated on a yearly basis) and regarding *kilayim* (making sure the seeds of their fields did not contain any forbidden mixtures)." What do these two mitzvos of giving a half shekel and *kilayim* have to do with one another? The Chidushei HaRim answers that the donation of the half shekel should be pure, it should not contain any other foreign mixture (intent and thought, *kilayim*). The Hebrew word *kilayim* comes from the same language of *"va'yikalei ha'am—and the people stopped giving."* There needs to be restraint and a holding back (not of the money, but rather) of the ulterior motives for which a person may give charity. By the giving of the half shekel, the Torah dictates that the rich cannot give more and the poor cannot give less. The wealthy person cannot give more because we are afraid his intentions may not be pure.

When we are told to live within our means, it is reflective of both our physical world and our spiritual world. With too much credit one can easily borrow too much and not be able to pay it back.

It's good to have the credit at your disposal, but you do not necessarily have to use it all up. In the realm of mitzvos and giving *tzedakah*, a person also must be careful in his "giving" lest he forget why he is giving. Every penny or half shekel must be entirely *l'shem Shamayim*—for Heaven's sake. It must be without a tinge of benefit in even the minutest way for the donor. The Jewish people were restrained in order to remind them to give for the right reasons and with proper motivation.

◆ ◆ ◆

Prayer is a pretty awesome concept, especially if you know what you're saying! A beautiful *tefillah* that we say on Shabbos morning between the Haftarah and putting away the Torah is *Yekum Purkan*. It concludes with a special blessing known as the *Mi SheBeirach* for those who dedicate their lives to learning, teaching, and giving, to uphold Torah. *Mi SheBeirach*, which translates as "The One Who blesses" is summarized as follows:

> *Particularly those who establish synagogues for prayer, and those who come to pray, those who give candles for lighting and wine for Kiddush and Havdalah, who give bread for the guests and charity for the poor. All who involve themselves in communal work with faith, HaKadosh Baruch Hu will reward and will remove all illness from them and heal their bodies, and forgive their sins and reward the work of their hands...*

This *tefillah* is designed for those who take care of community needs and the needy on a daily basis. Perhaps we need to substitute for some of those items, as they might be outdated. For example, few shuls solicit people to donate wine or candles for lighting, but general funds are collected and specific items are purchased with that money. When funds are collected on a personalized basis or directed for a specific purpose, it affords more satisfaction to the giver. Conceivably, the donating of wine and bread may be substituted for donating tissues, coffee, or *besamim* ("spices") to the shul. There are many detailed items that a shul offers to members, nonmembers, and wayfarers that do not constitute part of official synagogue services. In other words, this blessing is still available to anyone who wants to make use of it in today's day and age.

In Jewish thought, it's not how much you give—whether it's a lot or a little—as long as your heart is doing it for the sake of Heaven. The synagogue or shul of today is a *mikdash me'at*, a small sanctuary similar to the Mishkan ("the Tabernacle"). Our giving today resembles the giving of charity toward the Mishkan itself. We find a similar concept of giving in *parashas Pekudei*. In Shemos 40:34–35, the Torah states: *"Vi'yechas he'anan es Ohel Moed u'chvod HaShem malei es HaMishkan. V'lo yachol Moshe lavo el Ohel Moed, ki shachan alav he'anan, u'chevod HaShem malei es haMishkan."* —*The cloud covered the Tent of Meeting, and the glory of HaShem filled the Mishkan. And Moshe was not able to come to the Tent of Meeting, for the cloud rested upon it, and the glory of HaShem filled the Mishkan."* Why couldn't Moshe enter the Tent of Meeting?

The answer is actually very simple. Moshe could not enter because there was no room—HaShem filled the entire Mishkan. The real question is, Why and what caused HaShem to completely fill up the Mishkan, leaving no room for Moshe or anyone else for that matter? Rabbi Yaakov Aryeh of Rahdzmin explains that the Mishkan was full of *ahavas Yisrael*—the love of every Jew—and their monies were all from the most sincere place. The Jews donated from their hearts, as the Torah states *"kal nediv lev—all of the gifts from the heart,"* which was the solid and undying premise of the Jew. As a result of their eagerness to give from the depths of their hearts, God's Presence descended upon the area where such giving took place. There was no space that did not have the feel of giving from a Jew, and that is the greatest honor to HaShem. God wants to be present where such love between Jews takes place, thereby allowing no room for anything else. *Sefer MiMaayanos HaNetzach* explains that at that moment of totally selfless giving to the Mishkan, HaShem loved the Jews so much that He could not leave any area of the Mishkan devoid of His Divine presence. And so the honor of HaShem filled the Mishkan, leaving no space for anything else.

The *Shaar bas Rabim* asks, How do we understand HaShem filling up the Mishkan? Doesn't it say in *Tehillim* that the heavens are reserved for HaShem's dwelling? How is it possible for HaShem, Who is completely spiritual, Who dwells in heaven, to come down to earth and appear in a physical place?

He responds by comparing God's strength and existence to a piece of coal and a flame. The source of the heat, represented by the coal, is HaShem living in heaven, while the flame reaches out, even extending into the physical world, making its place in the Mishkan. The actual reason we refer to the *Shechinah* as God's Presence is because the root of that word means "to dwell." The words *shachen* ("a neighbor"), *Shechinah* ("God's Presence"), and Mishkan ("the Tabernacle"), all share the common root of *dwelling*.

The *Midrash Shemos Rabbah* 33:8 states that at the time HaShem spoke to Moshe about the details of the Mishkan, Moshe said to God, "Master of the Universe, are the Jewish people able to do this? Are they able to build the Mishkan?" *HaKadosh Baruch Hu* answered him, "Even *one* Jew is able to build the entire Mishkan." In *Shemos* 25:2 we see that the source to provide the means to build the Mishkan is derived from within each person's heart. It is sometimes the small change that makes the difference in a large campaign. If you try to fill up an empty space with big boulders and rocks, they will pile onto each other, but there will still be gaps between them. By contrast, when small rocks, pebbles, and dirt are used, all the cracks and crevices are packed, and the space is filled to near capacity. Do not underestimate the value of the small donations. They all add up, actually completing or filling the gaps between the large donations.

Who knows if it's the big donation or the many smaller donations that keeps a shul or a yeshivah open and providing all its services? The lesson of building the Mishkan is to understand the value and importance of the many donations of all sizes and the subsequent joy of HaShem, leading Him to occupy the Mishkan to the degree that even Moshe Rabbeinu could not squeeze in.

May we all appreciate and never underestimate the power of giving, no matter how big or small. Through such giving we will merit to see the building of the third Beis HaMikdash speedily in our days.

◆　◆　◆

Call it coincidence or fate, it created a stir of excitement within me. A few weeks ago, I was approached within days of two somewhat different and distinct opportunities. One opportunity was for spiritual gain and the other economic. Time has yet to determine if they have anything to do with each other or not.

The first opportunity came from a tourist who was visiting with us from Mexico City. He was truly amazed at our community, but could not believe that we did not have a *kollel* in our shul. He boasted that in Mexico City today there are about sixty different *kollelim*. The explosion of Torah learning in Mexico City has taken place during the last twenty-five to thirty years.

I said to him, "It takes a lot of money to run and sustain a *kollel*."

He replied, "*Berachah v'hatzlachah* ("blessing and success") will come through increased Torah learning in a city."

Many people have come through our doors and urged me to open a *kollel*, but this individual offered to help get it off the ground and to contribute. Before he left, he gave me his card and said, "When you are ready to start the *kollel*, I will give the first twelve thousand dollars!" Here is a man who is putting his money where his mouth is.

The second opportunity came in a phone call from a stockbroker who visited our shul many years ago and had kept my contact information. He offered me the potential of an IPO (initial public offering) that his company believed would be the biggest ever. Rumors had it that Facebook would be going public next year. He presented me with an offer to buy into this venture. Without going into details, one needed a minimum of $200,000 to invest with him, with the conceivable payoff being 100–200 times the investment.

I began thinking how one can become spiritually wealthy from a *kollel* or financially well-off from an incredible investment opportunity.

Of course, the obvious dream would be to have the money necessary to open and fund a *kollel* by myself. Unfortunately, there are no guarantees in the investing of physical money, but the investment in a spiritual opportunity will always give back something spiritual to the investor.

The Torah states in *Devarim* 11:26: "*R'ei Anochi nosein lifneichem ha'yom berachah u'klalah—Behold, I have placed before you a blessing and a curse.*" I came across a beautiful insight in *Otzer Chaim* (a collection of words of Torah). The author of a *sefer* called *VaYedaber Moshe* comments that not always is an abundance of wealth a blessing. Many times, wealth leads to arrogance, jealousy, competition, and the continuous drive to make more money. This blessing turns out to be a curse.

This concept also goes for Eretz Yisrael. When the Jewish people observe the Torah and fulfill the mitzvos, then the land of Israel is blessed; but any blessing that is not based upon God's will is not a blessing at all.

The reason the verse mentions the word *ha'yom* ("today") is to inform us that there are two kinds of days. There is a day of blessing and a day of cursing. The days of blessing are when the righteous live by the words of the *mishnah* in *Pirkei Avos*, "*Im lo achshav aimasai—If* not now, then when?" We need to grab as many mitzvos as possible *today!* We must grab another *tefillah*, another *daf* Gemara, another *chesed*, a little more *tzedakah*. There is no time to waste.

The day of the wicked is when people say, "Today let's party—for tomorrow we are going to die anyway." That being the case, that day will be a curse, not only for that particular day, but forever. It is up to the Bnei Yisrael to make the right choice and choose the day of blessing.

The Facebook investment would not give any return for a few years and no guarantees of making money at all. A *kollel* and community learning gives an immediate return and the Guarantor has never defaulted on the (reward) pay out.

The Baal HaTurim says that the words "*es ha'berachah asher tishme'u*" (*Devarim* 11:27) contains end letters that make up the word "Torah" (*tav, hey, reish,* and *vav*). In the merit of Torah, the blessings will come.

Maybe if we open up a *kollel* then we will all become rich spiritually— and even monetarily!

• • •

One of the greatest dreams that some people express is the day they will retire. Their entire working career is waiting for that day...the one that they don't have to get up for work. But the day a person thinks will be their greatest blessing may end up being their greatest curse! The verse in *Iyov* 5:7 states: "*Adam l'amal yulad—God created man to toil.*" *Sanhedrin* 99b explains that "toil" means to toil in learning Torah.

In a similar vein, my father-in-law Reb Tzvi Rosen (he should live and be well!) always remarks that "whatever HaShem blessed him with, he would rather spend for giving *tzedakah* and *simchahs* rather than it going to pay medical bills." If a person is going to "retire" his money from what he should be spending it on, then HaShem is going to force his hand to spend it on unpleasant things.

The lexicon of Hebrew is so vast that every word the Torah uses needs scrutiny. The Torah states: "*Va'yeishev Yaakov b'eretz m'gurei aviv b'eretz Canaan—And Jacob dwelled in the land that his father (Isaac) sojourned in, in the land of Canaan.*" A question is raised as to why the word "dwell" is used in regard to Yaakov and "sojourn" is used regarding his father Yitzchak? It should have said Yaakov sojourned or Yitzchak dwelled, but why the crossover?

The slightest of blemishes in our *Avos* is revealed to us by our Sages, and in this case, blame is placed upon Yaakov for his wanting to "retire" and just dwell in the land rather than "keep on working" and sojourning in this world like his father Yitzchak did. God said to Yitzchak in *Bereishis* 26:3: "*Gur ba'aretz ha'zos—Sojourn in this land,*" referencing the fact that this world is *not* the place to just sit back and dwell. Rather, this world is designed for working; the next world is reserved for dwelling and resting. Even though when HaShem said to Yitzchak "sojourn," it was in Israel! It was his homeland, and nevertheless HaShem said "sojourn" to teach us that in this world we must never stop moving and working.

We also see this same idea regarding Avraham Avinu. In *Bereishis* 23:4, Avraham said to the Bnei Cheis when buying the Me'aras HaMachpelah:

"Ger v'toshav anochi—A sojourner and a resident dweller am I among you." Avraham actually lived as a citizen there, but nevertheless he perceived himself as just passing through this world. This mentality was handed down to Yitzchak from Avraham, but Yaakov tried a slight variation of this lesson from his father.

At times, we forget the main reasons for our existence. Yaakov, on some level, aspired to a path that was deemed to be a departure from the designated toil; HaShem came and sent him a strong reminder. Yaakov thought he would retire from a life of trials and tribulations. He built a life with a large family and a big business for all the children to participate in. Yaakov survived the fight with his brother, Eisav, and his battle with his father-in-law, Lavan. He experienced the scandal of his daughter Dina being abducted and the international condemnation regarding Shimon and Levi killing out Shechem. Yaakov felt he had endured his challenges and looked forward to "retire" to uninterrupted immersion in learning and teaching Torah. He obviously was not interested in retiring to the golf course or to watch sports. But HaShem makes it clear: not in this world. The entire episode of Yosef and his brothers explodes as a lesson and a sharp cue that this world is not meant for rest!

The lesson is very simple, we are supposed to work and sojourn in the path of HaShem until the very last day of our life. We must remember that this world is only temporary and that while we are here, we must gather and grab the mitzvos that will ultimately bring us true rest in the World to Come. Whether in Eretz Yisrael or *chutz la'aretz* ("outside of Israel"), we should keep in mind the journey is not over and we must continue fighting those challenges in life. Children and family, employers and employees, livelihood and health are all issues we continue to battle...*this* is the definition of *life!*

◆   ◆   ◆

Every year around Rosh HaShanah, I wonder how my accounting system performed. In the Talmud, *Beitzah* 16a and *Rosh HaShanah* 16a, the Rabbis teach that man's income and his sustenance for the entire year are determined and apportioned for him on Rosh HaShanah. The spreadsheet lists our income and expenses; hopefully we can at least have a balanced budget at the end of the year. When I make some extra money, it's always easy to say that HaShem budgeted that in for me this year. The challenge is how to deal with out-of-the-ordinary expenses. Do we attribute them to our Rosh HaShanah budget or to something else?

Recently, I ran into a spate of unexpected, out-of-the-daily-routine expenses. When I was in New York on a pouring rainy day, I was handed an unnecessary and silly "No Standing Zone" parking ticket. I was only there for about 35 seconds and got a whopping fine of $115 (yes, the cost of living in New York is rather exorbitant). Prior to my last flight, I had been searching for a piece of hand luggage, and, when I found it, saw that it needed to be cleaned. Foolishly, I put it into the washing machine, causing the agitator to be ripped out. I just threw the hand luggage into the washer, not thinking if this was really a wise move. A few bucks later, after temporarily fixing the washing machine, I decided that perhaps washing machines are not designed to wash hand luggage. On my most recent trip, I rented a car too close to the date of my arrival. Although I knew of this trip weeks in advance, I forgot to rent a car at the time I booked the airline tickets. This omission cost me substantially more for my negligence. My final little extra expense came from my car door handle and window breaking, forcing me to enter the car from the passenger side and either climb over the middle console or flick open the driver's door while sitting in the front passenger's seat. Two little pieces of plastic that definitely did not cost more than three dollars ended up costing me over one hundred times more than that.

In *parashas Ki Savo*, the Torah delivers a horrific description of what can happen to the Jewish people if we do not follow the Torah and serve God properly. In Scripture, this is known as the *tochachah*—the public rebuke and curses of the Jewish people — which forms the core belief that if we turn against HaShem we will get punished. A more subtle approach is found in *Devarim* 28:47: "*Tachas asher lo avadeta es HaShem Elokecha b'simchah u've'tuv leivav mei'rov kol—Because you did not serve HaShem your God with gladness and with goodness of heart, out of an abundance of everything.*" Rav Chaim Volozhin teaches that serving HaShem without joy is equated to a servant serving his enemies. Since the Jews did not serve HaShem with joy and a merry heart, it is as if they served only their enemies.

Rabbi Simcha Bunim of Peshischa comments on the words from *Divrei HaYamim* (Chronicles) 16:10: "*Yismach lev mevakshei HaShem— Those who seek out God will have a joyful heart.*" He explains that the nature of an ordinary person is to be sad when he is seeking out an object that he has lost. Only when he finds the item he was looking for does he become happy. But when a person seeks out God, the opposite is true; the exercise and process of seeking and searching for HaShem is done in a state of happiness and joy.

One of the reasons that *Ki Savo* is read before Rosh HaShanah is to send a message that *if* the curses from this *parashah* were decreed, then we want to get rid of them before the end of the year in order to start fresh next year. "*Tichleh shanah mi'klaloseha*—the year should end its curses" speaks to us metaphorically as well as concretely. We must view all "supposed" curses—things that we think are bad—and end that perception. We must remove "the curse" of how we look at situations and view our circumstances through a positive lens, viewing this as a good thing, not a bad one.

Yeshayahu 55:6 says: "*Dirshu HaShem b'heematzo—Seek out HaShem where you will find Him.*" I suggest that the seeking out of HaShem will only be successful if we look for the good that HaShem is doing for us, understanding that, in reality, everything that HaShem does for us is good. The concept of seeking out HaShem does not mean looking for God, but rather seeing God in every situation—good or bad. We must concentrate on all the happenings of our lives, those which seem good and those which appear bad, understanding that *all* is for the good. Even the curses are meant to be good for us.

Let us try to end potential curses by seeking out HaShem. This act, in and of itself, will bring us joy. At times when challenging things happen, we contemplate whether this is a blessing or a curse. When things go wrong, we question how that can possibly be good. Is it a good thing or a bad thing, a curse or a blessing, when money is lost because of negligence or bad *mazal*.

The proper *hashkafah* ("outlook or philosophy") is to be happy and satisfied with any situation in life and to seek out the good. What sometimes seems to be an unnecessary (or foolish) expense in reality is an inexpensive way to realize how necessary those little unexpected expenses really are.

TZIBBUR MEANS "COMMUNITY." TZIBBUR IS AN ACRONYM FOR TZADDIKIM/ BEINONIM/RESHAIM–THE RIGHTEOUS/ AVERAGE/WICKED. THESE KINDS OF PEOPLE MAKE UP THE COMMUNITY THAT WE FOCUS ON TO ENHANCE AND MAKE BETTER.

CHAPTER SIX
COMMUNITY

Rabbi Chaim of Volozhin writes in his *sefer Nefesh HaChaim* (*shaar aleph, perek dalet*): "The Mishkan and the Beis HaMikdash contained all of the spiritual power and forces of the entire world. All of the rooms in the Temple and all of the holy utensils had mirror images of the same in the Temple in heaven. There exists a *Yerushalayim shel Maalah*—a heavenly city of Jerusalem—which houses this heavenly Temple. Directly beneath this city in heaven lies the earthly Jerusalem and its place for the Temple. Since the Temple was made from a prototype from heaven, it contained a unique sanctity and holiness. God, therefore, imbued the physical Beis HaMikdash in Yerushalayim with holiness. In the beginning of *parashas Terumah* God says: "*V'asu li Mikdash v'shachanti b'socham—Build for Me a Sanctuary so that I can dwell in them.*" So, too, every Jew's essence has the ability to be a place where God's holiness will permeate."

In today's world, with the absence of the Beis HaMikdash, God looks to find a permanent—yet mobile—place where His presence will reside. There are two: the *beis knesses* and the Jew. The *beis knesses* is made of physical material and remains set in its place. If one needs to find holiness and spirituality, it is found within the walls of this structure. The *beis knesses* resembles the Beis HaMikdash in terms of its symbolic permanent place in the world. As we all know, there are times when we cannot reach a shul in order to learn or daven. What is one supposed to do then in order to connect to God? The answer is that each of us is capable of becoming a Mishkan, a portable Temple that is built and taken apart as we travel. We are all travelers on our individual paths of life. And just like the Mishkan ("Tabernacle") always contained the *kedushah* ("holiness") of God's Presence even as it alternated between its erected state and traveling state, so too the Jewish people. The ever-present "wandering Jew" always maintains the ability to feel and to be close to God.

Chazal teach the concept that every shul is referred to as a *mikdash me'at*—a small Temple—which, in the time of the Mashiach, they and every *beis midrash* and yeshivah will be brought to Eretz Yisrael and exist alongside the third Beis HaMikdash. The modern-day portable sanctuary found within every Jew guarantees that when Mashiach comes, we will also be returned to Eretz Yisrael, to Yerushalayim, and to the place of the Holy Temple.

Portable phones, shavers, laptop computers, iPads, and even rechargeable batteries are part and parcel of our daily lives. These portable devices are amazing, but when they are used, they eventually run out of power and need to be recharged. The human body and the human spirit are no different. Whether it's our physical strength or our spiritual energy, we need to constantly touch back to the source of that energy and rejuvenate ourselves.

The key for every person to prosper and grow is to connect the inner portable sanctuary to the main source. The Jewish people cannot grow and flourish in isolation. We need to be closely linked to our primary source of energy, our communities, and our shuls. Maintaining a close relationship with these sources of vitality will afford longevity to the person's spiritual journey.

Get involved in your community and your shul. That's where we find God.

◆ ◆ ◆

The opening of *Devarim* has Moshe reviewing the history of the Jews in the desert. One of the major sticking points of rebuking the people was the story of the spies. One of the famous questions is, Why did Moshe give in to the people's request to send the spies? He should have flat-out refused, saying, "We cannot doubt HaShem."

The Malbim explains that Moshe was *dan le'kaf zechus*—he judged them favorably by allowing them *"la'tur es ha'aretz*—to visit the land." He did not think they would "spy out the land," in its negative connotation. In 1:23, there is a repetition of the words "one man per tribe." The full verse states: *"Va'yitav b'einai ha'davar va'ekach mi'kem shneim asar anashim—The idea was good in my (Moshe's) eyes, so I took from you twelve men, one man for each tribe."* Could we not assume that the twelve men would come one from each tribe? The fact is that the word "spies" connotes at least two together. Rather, each tribe is sending only one person, indicating that they were not spies; they were more like tourists. Unfortunately, they banded together and set out to form a group of spies.

This was not the first time in history (and it was not the last time either) that a leader sent someone ahead of the nation to check something out. At the end of *Bereishis*, prior to Yaakov Avinu going down to live in Egypt, he sent his son Yehuda to Yosef so he would show him Goshen. Rashi refers to the Midrash which states that the reason he sent him ahead of the family was to establish a house of learning, a yeshivah. Yaakov Avinu's lesson to all of his children, current and future, is that wherever we travel in the world, we need to establish a place and a time to learn Torah. The only way for a house in Israel to sustain itself is by making it a place of Torah. Building a home filled with Torah values is easier when we are surrounded by the entire Torah-observant community.

Perhaps Moshe was just following the advice of his forefather Yaakov, who demonstrated that before we go in as a nation, we must first send individuals to lay the foundation of Torah in the land. The Noam Elimelech, Rav Elimelech Weisblum, reinforces this idea by explaining an incredible *segulah* in the service of God: to always have trustworthy friends who will help. In order for a person to truly serve the Almighty, one cannot do it alone. We cannot serve God by being the only one.

Without any friends and support, we can never be able to truly serve HaShem. Every community needs a good *sevivah* (environment). This is clearly evident in communities that boast *kollelim*, outreach professionals, and the like. When children and adults have more role models around them, they are able to reach greater spiritual heights. I, for one, receive a boost in the summertime when we host a SEED program, have a camp in our neighborhood, and experience an inundation of observant Jews who come to San Diego. There is electricity in the air and a buzz of learning, davening, and all-around spiritual growth. Jews from all walks of life, the full spectrum of religious Jews, descend upon San Diego, the community and our shul.

Make an effort to surround yourself with more "Torah personalities." Role models are one of the keys to a successful community. The more *rabbe'im* in the schools, the more outreach professionals on campus, the more youth directors there are in town, will ultimately shape each and every one of us in our building a strong relationship with HaShem. This, in turn, will hopefully stimulate the Jewish people to learn more Torah, to treat each other with greater respect, and to deserve the coming of Mashiach speedily in our days.

◆ ◆ ◆

Everyone has certain memories of different stages in his life. One of my fondest memories regarding my days in Yeshiva Shaarei Torah was watching a true *gadol* ("Torah giant") walk into the *beis midrash* every morning for Shacharis. Rav Yosef Zvi Aronson, *zt"l*, would come in, reciting out loud: "*Mah tovu ohalecha Yaakov mishkenosecha Yisrael*—How goodly are your tents, O Jacob, your dwelling places, O Israel" (*Bamidbar* 24:5).

At barely five feet tall, he entered, swaying side to side, rubbing his hands together as he walked toward his seat on the *mizrach* (the front of the shul where the rabbis sit). The *bachurim* ("students") of the yeshivah did not fully appreciate who this "giant" of a man was. We really did not interact with him except when he made a *siyum* ("completion") on a tractate every few months, at which time we were treated to a great breakfast. I still recall the hum of the words "*Mah tovu*" called out in a low, raspy voice upon the Rav's setting foot in the *beis midrash*. If I was lucky enough to say those words as I scurried to my seat, I would have been happy. The Rav, on the other hand, was totally absorbed in their meaning and message. One could only imagine that the author of those words was some great Jew and would never even guess that they actually came from the mouth of the non-Jewish prophet Bilaam.

Today, we customarily say these words as we enter the shul, but what is their significance?

There are many commentaries (seventy *panim* ["faces"] to be exact) that address every detail of the Torah. Some are on a simple, mundane level, while others contain deep, kabbalistic messages. It is our nature to look for the silver lining, even when learning about a seemingly negative occurrence. It is fascinating that evil Bilaam's words are so precious to us. Consider the background: Balak, the king of Moav, hires Bilaam, a non-Jewish prophet, to curse the Jewish nation. We are familiar with the story that his attempt to curse the Jews is reversed, becoming instead a blessing. On the surface this seems to be virtuous and to be honest—most commentaries agree that the words of Bilaam came out as a blessing and not as the intended curse.

On the other hand, there is a story which reveals that some of the words of Bilaam's blessings were really a curse in disguise. *Sanhedrin* 105a states that when the Jewish people sin, then all of the evil thoughts of Bilaam will be fulfilled except for one: the shuls and yeshivahs will never cease to exist—forever. Once again, on the surface this appears to be a blessing. And yet...

In 1859, when Rav Shimon Sofer arrived in Cracow to become the head of the Beis Din, he was alarmed to find over one hundred synagogues and *shteiblach*; he understood clearly that this represented a lack of *shalom* and harmony among the Jews of Cracow. He commented that he now fully understood the meaning of Bilaam's words and his attempt to curse the Jews. According to the Rabbis, Bilaam wanted to curse the Jews, but God would not let him. Instead, HaShem put the words of *Mah Tovu* onto Bilaam's tongue. We see that what Bilaam actually said (the blessing) did not match what was in his heart, so therefore none of the "curses or blessings" came true. However, this blessing of *Mah Tovu* and the abundance of places the Jews daven and learn *could* be interpreted as a dysfunction, and, therefore, a disunity of the Jewish people. To this, Bilaam agreed fully in his heart and in his words. Because the action of speaking and the intent of Bilaam's heart were consistent, this (and only this) "blessing" would always remain. Rav Sofer now understood the Gemara and lamented over the state of affairs for the Jewish people.

One of our greatest challenges is maintaining close-knit communities and shuls for people from a variety of diverse backgrounds. Can we not live together? Must we only interact with people *exactly* like us? It is not easy to maintain the sense of "oneness" in a diverse community, but it is essential. This is the true blessing of which Bilaam would have no part. We must come together to learn, to pray, and even to socialize. And that brings the majesty and the power of the blessing, "*How goodly is our tent, O Jacob, our dwelling place, O Israel!*"

May we all be blessed with the vision of *Am Yisrael k'ish echad b'lev echad!*

◆ ◆ ◆

When a person is in the comfort of his home, he is surrounded by all of the physical and material possessions that give him pleasure. His worldly contentment can keep his mindset far from the aspiration to bring a sacrifice to the Holy Temple. But once he reaches the entrance way to the Tent of Meeting and sees the Holy Temple and witnesses the *Kohanim* who are involved in the service, his feelings immediately change. Instantly, he feels emotionally overwhelmed by the opportunity of offering a sacrifice and being part of this incredible experience. His attitude is now totally altered. The verse (in *Vayikra* 1:3) indicates this with the word *lirtzono*, understood as "voluntarily." He now brings that very same *korban* with total *kavanah* ("concentration"). Arriving at the Beis HaMikdash is enough to change a person's approach in the service to HaShem. (This idea can be extended to every mitzvah; we often have to push ourselves to do them. Even though we may start out in a belligerent fashion, once we come to the threshold of performing the mitzvah, our initial resistance is transformed to a strong desire to accomplish the task at hand.)

Once a person gets to shul, the ambiance of the shul and the beauty of the davening will transform the individual from feeling forced to come to shul to becoming a willing participant, to have a strong desire to pray. There are times when the services are a bit too slow or a little too fast for our pace. There are times when the temperature in the synagogue is either a bit too warm or too cold for our comfort. Yes, there are times when there might be too much chatter or the rabbi's sermon was too long for your particular listening pleasure. Nevertheless, a person must put forth the effort to understand that prayer, for Jews, is communal; we are each an integral part of the group. Davening is not just about me and what I like. We need to have others in mind and particularly to understand that each of us is part of an interconnected group. The very act of coming to shul encourages us to *want* to daven.

◆ ◆ ◆

Why do people come to shul? Whether for services, or for a *shiur*, or some event, the following is only a partial list:

- My spouse forced me to go.
- A Kiddush (free food/socializing with friends and arguing with enemies/having a place for my kids to run around and wreak havoc—at least it's not my house!).
- To get away from my kids and home responsibilities.
- Because I've been doing it all my life; I have nothing else to do.
- Maybe I actually come to daven to HaShem!

Once it has been determined why people attend shul, the next step is to learn how often they go. The range of attendance is from every day to only going on Shabbos, to going for an event or holiday. Even those who only go on Shabbos tend to be a bit choosy—they may select

Friday night or Shabbos morning, but never all three of the services.

Perhaps I grew up in a different generation, but Shabbos was a time when everybody went to shul—all three times. During the week, people are busy and have poor excuses, but, nevertheless, at least there is an excuse. However, why are there excuses in the first place for many who really could go to shul? The answer lies in the poor understanding and lack of appreciation for what davening and communal prayer accomplishes for a person and his family.

Everything comes from HaShem. We need to put ourselves in a situation which allows us to seek Him out.

Eisav and Yaakov are described as a man of the field and a man of the tent, respectively. *"Va-yigdlu ha-ne'arim va-yehi Eisav ish yodayah tzayid ish sadeh, v'Yaakov ish tam yosheiv ohalim."* It says that Yaakov was a *yosheiv ohalim* ("sat in tents")—plural. The *Midrash Bereishis Rabbah* 63 explains that these were the tents of different study halls. First, Yaakov studied with his grandfather, Avraham. Then he studied in the yeshivah of Shem, and then he continued on to learn in the yeshivah of Eiver. *Midrash Rabbah* 48:8 points out that Shem and his great grandson Eiver had separate yeshivahs. Yaakov felt it necessary to learn in different yeshivahs at different points in his life. Rav Yehuda Loewy, the Maharal from Prague, explains that Rivka sought advice from Shem about her difficult pregnancy. Yaakov eventually left the study hall of Shem and went off to learn with Eiver, who was obviously much younger than his great grandfather. The Maharal derives from here that a person can learn from anybody, even a younger person or a person of lesser stature. The most important component of deepening one's knowledge is to learn from someone who speaks to your heart. A person does not have the merit to learn from anybody. Rather, we each need to learn from a person who is specifically suited to our unique learning needs, even if that individual may not be the best or most famous Rebbi.

The merits of Yaakov Avinu are highlighted in *Midrash Rabbah* 63:2. This Midrash tells us that Avraham Avinu was saved from the furnace Nimrod tossed him into due to the merit of Yaakov sitting in his tent! Yaakov's greatness was not only that the world knew of his good deeds, but that he would only show his good ways when necessary. The description of him as an *ish tam*—a wholesome, perfect individual—is that his speech was like his heart. Yaakov was humble and modest. He made sure to shepherd his father's sheep and to sit in the tent of Torah. *Midrash Rabbah* 65:17 describes Yaakov's physical prowess as greater than Eisav's (an image that is the antithesis of our perception of Yaakov). His two arms were like two pillars of marble. No person could physically stand up against Yaakov, but he never displayed this strength unless it was absolutely necessary to fight his enemies—he preferred the tents.

The *Sifsei Kohen*, which was also called the *Shach*, says: "Yaakov's tents were the beginning of it all, because from then on, the Jewish people would have a place to ask and request their needs and aspirations, believing that HaShem was listening to their *tefillos*. The study halls and synagogues are where God resides." Therefore, we converge there multiple times a day, making them our central places in life. Rabbi Abba in the Talmud says about Bilaam's curses that all the blessings will revert back to curses with the exception of the shuls and yeshivahs. As it states: "...that HaShem will turn the curse into a blessing, only a single curse." This tells us that as long as there are shuls and yeshivahs, there will not be any curses. (*Shaarei Aharon*, vol. 12, p. 915)

Yaakov Avinu's incredible strength was centered on the building and maintaining of his tents for himself and for his future family. The tents that Yaakov pitched were physically strong and spiritually sound. I am sure Yaakov's tents provided a great Kiddush, were beautifully designed, had a place for children to play, and also welcomed guests who came to socialize from all over the world. The primary purpose, however, was to establish a place where a person could receive nourishment as well as nurture a relationship with HaShem that would endure. Yaakov ultimately created a place that our *neshamos* yearn for in order to get closer to HaShem.

Let us work to create the "tents" that our forefather Yaakov intended them to be.

◆　◆　◆

After learning in yeshivah and preparing to become a pulpit rabbi, I was asked a question that completely threw me off course. I certainly was well prepared to handle all kinds of questions, from the basic to the complex. My *semichah* ordination covered the laws of family purity, Shabbos, kashrus, festivals, mourning, and all other life-cycle events. We were trained for the most difficult situations and to figure out what the proper and appropriate decision would be through analytical derivation.

I was caught off guard when asked a very basic question that, in yeshivah, we really took for granted and did not really ever expect to be asked. "Rabbi, what do I get for my membership?" Such a profound question floored me and I was totally flustered. This they surely did not teach us in rabbinical school! Where does one find or even begin to look for the answer to such a question?

So the obvious address was Rabbi Wein, my *rosh yeshivah*. After all, it was he who trained us for the rabbinate; he surely would have the answer. After mustering up the courage to ask him such a question, he replied without blinking an eye or taking a breath. He said, "Membership to a shul entitles you to a place to daven." A shul is not the Jewish community center where we have swimming, social events, basketball, and everything secular and nothing religious. To the contrary, a synagogue is a place of spirituality, where we connect emotionally and spiritually to God. We may have some benefits of the social element at times, such as during Kiddush and *Shalosh Seudos*. We also cater to activities and programs for the young and old, but that is not the main objective of a shul. A shul is a place to daven—a place where we can connect with our Creator.

There are more than fifteen Hebrew words that describe prayer. One of them is *va'eschanan*—"*Va'eschanan el HaShem...*" This wording was used when Moshe implored God to let him enter into Eretz Yisrael. A derivation of the word *va'eschanan* is *chinun*, which comes from the word "free." The Sages tell us that Moshe was asking for a *matnas chinam* ("a free gift"), something above and beyond what he deserved. There is a storehouse filled with "free gifts" for us; in order to receive them, all we need to do is ask.

Moshe Rabbeinu is teaching us what membership entitles us to. We gather together in a *beis knesses* to daven and ask HaShem for those precious things that we need, even if we do not deserve them. One could ask, If we do not deserve them, then why would God give them to us?"

The answer lies in the word *va'eschanan*, whose numerical value equals 515, the number of times that Moshe recited this prayer in order to be allowed to go into Israel. At this point, HaShem told Moshe to stop and not ask even one more time; otherwise He would have to give in to Moshe and grant his request. We therefore see that our *tefillos*, when repeated over and over again, greatly affect the outcome. And even if we do not deserve that which we ask for, God considers and often grants us our requests.

Socializing might be great, but don't forget to pray—with all your heart.

◆　◆　◆

Mitzvah no. 612 is named *"Hakhel."* Once every seven years, the Jewish people are commanded to gather in Jerusalem to hear the king read from certain sections of the Torah. In *Devarim* 31:12, it states: *"Hakhel es ha'am ha'anashim v'hanashim v'hataf v'gercha asher biusharecha l'maan yishmeu u'lmaan yilmdu v'yaru es HaShem Elokeichem v'shamru laasos es kol divrei haTorah hazos—Gather together the people—the men and the women and the small children, and the stranger who is in your cities—so that they will hear and so that they will learn, and they shall fear HaShem, your God, and be careful to perform all the words of this Torah."*

Rashi, based on *Chagigah* 3a, comments that it was necessary to bring the children in order to give reward to those who brought them!

In truth, we know that quite often younger children cause a ruckus in shul and disturb the adults. As a result of their noisemaking,[2] people cannot hear or pay attention to the services. This begs the question, If the young children are going to make noise, why bring them to shul? Why go through the trouble of bringing them if they are going

---

2   Incidentally, the children's noise is without intent or without a sense of knowing better—as opposed to the adults who make noise and should know better.

to require attention and distract their parents and others during the services? Would we not be better off if we just left our children at home, so as not to disturb our service to God?

Rav Nasson HaKohen Adler (1741–1800), a German kabbalist born in Frankfurt, explains that not only is there great reward in bringing young children to shul, he states that "the reward is greater than the loss." Children get excited when they come to shul, and it makes an everlasting impression upon their hearts, creating a desire to serve HaShem. Bringing children who will likely need tending to reaps more benefits for the parent even though their davening or learning will likely be interrupted. Obviously, a parent has a responsibility to make sure that the child does not disturb others. There is a fascinating *halachah* which instructs that a parent is permitted to interrupt his Amidah in order to take care of his child and then resume his *tefillah* from the place where he stopped, even if he broke from the stance of his feet being together.[3] I am not aware of any other time or situation a person is allowed to interrupt davening the Shemoneh Esrei and then resume where he left off. Usually, Halachah dictates that if you move your feet apart and interrupt your Shemoneh Esrei, you need to start over again from the beginning. Of course, if a person can control the situation without moving from his place, he should try to do so.

Rav Adler concludes his thought by saying, "There is a tremendous lesson to be gleaned from this. A person is better off deflecting some of his personal growth in order to educate his children properly in Torah and good deeds."

It is so upsetting that in today's day and age many parents tend not to bring their children to shul on a regular basis. Parents think that they are entitled to a break and therefore avoid having to deal with their children, preferring to leave them at home when they go to shul. Remember, there is no vacation from parenting. It's a 24/7 job! It is imperative, however, that children sit next to one of their parents so that the parent will be a role model and demonstrate how one should behave in shul. While some parents think they need a break, others feel

---

3   *Tefillah k'Hilchasah*, pp. 247–248, footnotes 200–205.

they cannot daven properly with their young, fidgety children making noise or causing problems. God, through the mitzvah of *Hakhel*, is telling us not to worry about our own davening or needing to take a break. The most important issue is bringing children to shul and dealing with them—even at our own spiritual expense.

Unfortunately, there are many shuls that encourage parents to leave their children at home until they are old enough to know how to behave. I believe that this can create a serious disconnect—both for the children and for their parents. Children need to develop a positive relationship by attending shul, and the only sure way to nurture this relationship is through shul attendance.

We must decide on a case-by-case at what age it is appropriate to bring a child to shul. Be aware that whatever age your child is, you must be ready and willing to sacrifice some of your own davening time in order to teach, guide, and train your child to be in shul. Let's see to it that our children sit with us, learn from us how we are supposed to behave in shul, and share with them a positive experience in their *avodas HaShem*.

◆ ◆ ◆

We have focused considerably on the shul, but, the truth is, communities need other things as well. The Torah states: *"Va'yeishev Yaakov b'eretz m'gurei aviv b'Eretz C'naan—And Yaakov settled in the land of his father's sojourning, in the land of Canaan."* Rabbeinu Bachya explains that the word *va'yeishev* connotes dwelling in a holy place. The holy place is Eretz Yisrael, the land in which his father and grandfather sojourned. His forefathers were uprooted from Eiver HaNahar and ended up sojourning in the land of Israel.

Yaakov intended to live out the rest of his life in holiness and spirituality, just as Avraham and Yitzchak had done. *Va'yeishev* does not only mean to live in the physical sense, it also refers to living in the spiritual sense, in the manner in which our *Avos* lived. Our forefathers built a spiritual and holy place to live around them. Yaakov wanted to do the same thing at the end of his life. He created an atmosphere around him and his family which enabled him to serve HaShem and to demonstrate for all future generations what it takes to live in a thriving Jewish community.

I was recently asked a question regarding what it takes to have young families thrive in a small community. There are a few basic concepts that must be considered when answering this question. Moving to a community is like finding a *shidduch*—not every community will be a fit for every person. Some people need to be in a big city, while others prefer and thrive in a smaller one. A sign of a growing community is having young families move in and stay. The question is, What will convince them to move in...and then to stay?

A young couple may come to appreciate the value of a smaller town. They may appreciate life without the rat race and the need to keep up with high standards of *gashmiyus* ("physical pleasures and conveniences") that are found in some of the larger Jewish communities. However, they should be prepared physically and mentally for the fact that moving to a smaller community is not all about taking. To be part of a smaller community, one is required to give, to be involved in the building and growing process. One does not have to be a Rebbi or an outreach professional to give to the community. One can be a good *baal habayis* and become a strong part of the community.

Often, young couples will come to a community with either no children or very young children. At that point, the *chinuch* in the community is still satisfactory for their needs. Sometimes, however, they begin to outgrow the Day School system and want more than the community can provide. The family will eventually reach a crossroads and need to determine whether or not they feel they can continue to grow and reach the next level locally or will have to move to a larger Jewish community. I believe that usually, with the proper resources, they will be able to rise up and be ready to join the ranks of mainstream yeshiva high schools, coming from a smaller city.

This situation particularly applies to a *kollel* couple or an outreach professional, who will be okay until their children reach a certain point. Therefore, if the community is not moving forward, they will leave.

Unfortunately, they have to realize that being part of a community is not about themselves, but rather it is about the greater good for everyone else. If their family can grow within this challenge, they will benefit greatly; if not, they will not stay.

In order to build a community, two things are needed. First, the community needs to clearly want people to stay, and second, the people must want to stay. "Want" means that one is willing to sacrifice to attain one's goals. If someone really wants something, he will figure out how to make it work. If either the wife or husband cannot sacrifice, then they should not move to an "out-of-town" community. Everybody prioritizes things that they want and need out of life. Nobody in any community, large or small, gets everything they want. It's always a compromise— matter of what one is willing to give up in order to receive.

From the community's side, there has to be some basic infrastructure. A full-time Day School, a shul, a *mikveh*, and some kosher food available through restaurants and supermarkets. A positive sign in seeking out a community is stability. Long-standing institutions in a community are strong attractions to families thinking about living there. If a community cannot support a Day School or a shul, or if it changes rabbis as often as they change light bulbs, then I would stay away from considering that location.

In addition, everyone in the community has to be willing to invest money, time, and effort in order to foster a Torah-learning and a Torah-living environment. Not everyone has money, but most people can give time and effort. They must foster a feeling that they are trying to grow. Communities that are actively pursuing and hiring more staff— i.e., college *kiruv* professionals and youth directors—and initiating programs such as Partners in Torah, demonstrate an active community. A community must confirm its commitment to growth, sharing its excitement and enthusiasm in order to attract young couples who want to join something that is already developing. People want to be a part of success, not failure.

In order for young families to want to remain in their communities or to attract new young families to move in, a community must provide both *ruchniyus* and *gashmiyus*. Let each of us build our communities, just as our forefathers Avraham, Yitzchak, and Yaakov did in their generations.

Each individual counts and is appreciated—let's make sure everyone feels it!

◆　◆　◆

One sign of artistic maturity is the process of learning to understand, appreciate, and enjoy the finer things in life. It takes a refined eye and astute perception to recognize and appreciate finesse, grace, and beauty. As an avid sports fan, I truly believe that genuine grace and beauty, on the highest level, can be found in sporting performances. Whether it is coordinated efforts on a team level directed by a skillful manager or coach, or just the incredible efforts made on an individual level by athletes, there is considerable talent that is exhibited on the field. However, sports are not usually held up as classic examples where one can witness finesse, grace, and beauty. Usually, that concept is associated with museums, concerts, plays, etc., which I rarely attended in my youth. I guess the following piece is a sign of my aging.

I recently attended a cantorial concert which included a phenomenal orchestra. Of all the performers, the singers, and the musicians, there was one person who, on the surface, appeared to not be doing very much.

The maestro or conductor stands on a podium and waves a baton which, to the untrained eye, seems not only pretty easy, but also appeared to me—a novice in this area—to be rather useless. As I began to observe him more carefully, focusing on his every move, I could detect the attention he garnered from every one of the musicians and singers. I noticed that throughout the performance they looked to him for guidance and direction.

Conducting is the art of directing a musical performance by way of visible gestures; it is also the art of bringing the musicians to a new level of understanding and expression of the music. The primary duties of the conductor are to unify the performers, set the tempo, execute clear preparations and beats, and to listen critically to each instrument, shaping the overall sound of the ensemble. Conductors are more than guides to the orchestras or choirs that they conduct; they are interpreters. They choose the works to be performed, study the scores (the full orchestral notations of the symphonic piece), work out their interpretation, and relay those interpretations to the performers. In addition, the conductor demands absolute obedience in every detail of that interpretation from every musician in the orchestra. Orchestras, choirs, concert bands, and other sizable musical ensembles have conductors. Small ensembles such as quartets have one musician as the lead, who the others follow.

The Mishkan (Tabernacle) was *l'havdil* an edifice that had a "show" that needed to be performed with perfection and unanimity. Let's consider the *bigdei Kehunah*—the Priestly garments. Four specific, unique garments were worn during the *avodah* ("service") by an ordinary *Kohen* while the *Kohen Gadol*—the High Priest—wore an additional four garments during his service, particularly on Yom Kippur. One of those four additional pieces was the *tzitz*, a gold band worn on the forehead that had the words "*Kodesh laHashem*" on it. Many commentaries mention that the *tzitz* was not actually a garment, but rather an accessory.

Rabbi Yosef Chaim of Bahgdad writes in his *sefer*, the *Ben Ish Chai*, how the Jewish people stem from one place and we are like one body. Kabbalisticaly, the word *tzitz*, spelled *tzadi* (equals 90), *yud* (equals 10), and *tzadi* again (equals 90, but can be expanded to count as 900) represents the number 1,000, corresponding to the years that Adam HaRishon was supposed to have lived. After the sin, the 1,000 was broken up as follows: 90 went up to the upper spheres, 10 remained on earth, and the remaining 900 fell to the *klipos*—"spiritual shells around the world." The Torah states: "*V'asisa tzitz zahav tahor, u'fitachta alav pituchei chosam Kodesh La'HaShem—You shall make a tzitz of pure gold, and you shall engrave upon it like the engraving of a signet, 'Holy to HaShem.'*" The *tzitz*, as Rashi explains, was like a golden plate that was two fingerbreadths wide, extending around the forehead from ear to ear. Along with the Torah that was written as **the blueprint for** the world and therefore predated Creation, HaShem also had to have thought about a people who would accept and follow the Torah. That *machshavah* ("thought") was the souls of the Jewish people—conceived of prior to the creation of the world along with the Torah. The *tzitz* was worn on the forehead of the *Kohen Gadol*, since the forehead is opposite the place where thinking occurs in the brain.

The *Zohar HaKadosh* in *Vayakhel* 218 explains that the *tzitz* rested on the forehead so that when the Jewish people saw it on the *Kohen Gadol*, it would *"break their hearts and remind them of the purity from whence they came."* Anyone who looked at the *tzitz* became embarrassed about his sins and ultimately repented. This was an added effect which the *tzitz* had on the Jewish people. It reminded us where we came from and the source which reveals that we Jews are all one. This was accomplished through the *Kohen Gadol*—who in reality was the maestro or the conductor for the entire Jewish people. The *Kohen Gadol*, as the conductor, is able to coordinate and bring every player in the choir or orchestra together, reminding each one of them that they are part of this special group called the Jews.

The Jewish people as a whole are compared to a symphony. If one musician is out of tune, plays the wrong note, or misses a cue from the conductor, the entire piece is ruined. Precision and accuracy is necessary for each and every member of the orchestra. The conductor, therefore, must be in complete control. He works very diligently to create the sound and cohesiveness that makes a performance memorable. Each and every Jew is part of HaShem's orchestra. In order for the world to hear a beautiful symphony of life, it is incumbent upon every Jew to play his part flawlessly. Just as each member of the orchestra, along with every person attending a concert, looks to the conductor to attain deeper understanding of a piece of music, so too, every Jew needs to look toward our Conductor. During Temple times, we were able to look to the *Kohen Gadol* for leadership, but today we lack such a person. Therefore, we need to find great *gedolim*—leaders of our people—who will help us coordinate our lives to play the right music at the right time.

◆ ◆ ◆

From time to time, I get stopped in grocery stores and parking lots by gentiles who see the black velvet yarmulke on my head and ask me, "Are you Jewish?" I wonder if women wearing a burka are asked if they are Muslim.

Nevertheless, when asked if I am Jewish, I proudly reply yes. My response is usually followed by statements such as, "I love the Jewish people," "I've been to Israel," "I support Israel," "I have Jewish friends," "I love kosher food," etc.

Interestingly, across the country in New York, as I waited on the security line at JFK Airport, I could also pick out the Jews—both male and female. Whether a woman was wearing a sheitel, tichel, or was just appropriately dressed, she stood out from the crowd. Similarly, a man who was wearing any type of head covering or was just dressed like a Jew was easy to spot. Despite having these Jews in plain sight, I did not notice anyone approaching them—or me either, for that matter—and asking if we were Jewish.

What is the obvious difference between the Jews in New York versus my home in San Diego?

The Jewish people have been wandering from exile to exile, from one country to the next. What is the key to raising children in the *galus* and to maintain their connection to Hashem?

Moshe's two sons were named Gershom and Eliezer. In *Shemos* 18:3, the Torah states: "*V'eis shnei baneha asher sheim ha'echad Gershom ki amar ger hayisi b'eretz nachriyah—And the name of her two sons, of whom the name of one was Gershom, for he had said, 'I was a sojourner in a strange land.'*" The very next verse states: "*V'sheim ha'echad Eliezer ki Elohei ahvi b'ezree va'yatzilainee mei'cherev Paroh—And the name of the one was Eliezer, for the God of my father came to my aid, and He saved me from the sword of Pharaoh.*" Rabbeinu Bachya (some pronounce it Bechaye) claims that on this latter verse the Torah should have said, "And the name of the *second* son was..." Why does it repeat "one" and not indicate that Eliezer was the second son?

Quoting from the *Pesikta D'Zrutrasa*, the first "one" was specific to his mother; the latter "one" was specific to his father. Gershom, who was the firstborn, was specific to his mother. Perhaps she had the right to name their first child. (This could be the source for today's *minhag* that the mother gets to name the first child.) Moshe got to name the second child Eliezer, thanking HaShem for saving him, hence the name Eli ("my God"), and Ezer ("helping me").

Rabbeinu Bachya gives another insight regarding the word *echad*— one. Eliezer had extra strength through his oneness. This oneness represents *achdus*—unity. Later on in history, God would influence the power of Eliezer through his one and only son Rechavya. Rechavya is mentioned in *Divrei HaYamim* (Chronicles I 23:17): "*And the sons of Eliezer were: Rechavya the chief, and Eliezer had no other sons, but the sons of Rechavya multiplied greatly (rabu l'maalah)."* The Ralbag explains they "multiplied greatly" as referring to more than the usual birth rate. *Berachos* 7a expounds on the words *rabu l'maalah* as meaning above or more than the 600,000. Eliezer was the progenitor of a similar number of people, as what we were in Egypt. Therefore, the verse intentionally uses the word "one" to indicate the power and influence of even *one* person. From the one—Eliezer—came 600,000 people. The Malbim explains they were of great stature and were entrusted with the vast wealth of the Temple treasuries, a fortune entrusted only to men of the highest character.

The uniqueness of one individual has the potential to create magnificent things in this world. Often in life, we view the second of something as nothing more than a repeat of the first and therefore do not treat it as something unique and special. I sometimes feel that the Jewish view on Jews of the world is categorized, placing Jews living in the major cities as primary and Jews living in other second- or third-tier cities as secondary-type Jews. If my perception is accurate (you could disagree), this is a very unfortunate situation for Klal Yisrael. Every single Jew is not only seen equally in the eyes of HaShem, each and every individual must feel as strong and as essential as every other Jew—anywhere else in the world.

The Jew in New York may be viewed as Gershom, the firstborn of Moshe. The second son, Eliezer, represents Jews who live elsewhere, though we must remember that we are also the "one" and similar to the firstborn. "Out-of-town" Jews may serve a more important and significant role as the representatives of the Jewish people to gentiles, who really do not know what a Jew is all about.

The responsibility of the Jews living "out-of-town" lies in the potential of becoming a *Rechavya*—the forebearer of thousands of Jews who will follow us. An extra degree of responsibility falls on our shoulders to represent the Jewish people and to make sure we are on our best behavior in following the Torah and, of course, secular law as good, law-abiding citizens. Hopefully, through our actions, we can also create a following of 600,000 and become the leaders of the Jewish people who will take us out from the final exile and return us all to Eretz Yisrael with the coming of *Mashiach Tzidkeinu bimheirah b'yameinu.* Amen!

◆ ◆ ◆

Good guys and bad guys are always in the script. Rare is the story where the potential good guys come out smelling bad. Even though the deaths of Nadav and Avihu had already been recorded in *parashas Shemini*, nevertheless, the Torah states again in *Vayikra* 16:1: "*Va'yidaber HaShem el Moshe acharei mos shnei bnei Aharon, b'karvasam lifnei HaShem va'yamusu—HaShem spoke to Moshe after the death of Aharon's two sons, when they approached before HaShem and they died.*" Why is recording their death so important?

There are many reasons given regarding what warranted the deaths of Nadav and Avihu. The *Midrash Chachamim* says the primary source of their sin was that despite the fact that they were great and righteous leaders, they convinced themselves that they were getting closer to God. A true tzaddik always works on himself, raising his level to grow ever closer to HaShem. This effort does not come automatically with greatness. The greater a person becomes, the more he has to contend with the natural tendency to grow haughtier.

Nadav and Avihu were trying to act for the sake of Heaven, but the rule in life is one must do things that the *tzibbur* or majority of the people do. We cannot simply make up our own rules or even to decide to follow a Halachah unless we hold or accept the majority opinion. Many Halachos are mentioned and brought down, but we do not necessarily follow and act in accordance with that authority. Any individual, no matter how great he or she may be, cannot decide to follow a particular law that is outside the accepted viewpoint. The following *mishnah* discusses a powerful, strongly worded opinion consistent with this thought.

The first *mishnah* of the fourth chapter of *Pesachim* states: "In a place where the custom is to allow work on Erev Pesach until *chatzos* ("halachic midday"), they can do work. In a place where the custom is not to do work, the individual must conform to the public-at-large and refrain from doing *melachah* ("work"). Rashi explains that the reason the Sages instituted this fence was to assure that the people would not forget to do *biur chametz*, slaughter the *korban Pesach*, and arrange to have matzos for the evening Seder. From the statement of this *mishnah* we derive that it only depended upon the custom of the place until midday; that is where the difference took place. But after *chatzos*—midday—it is actually forbidden as a law and not just as a custom. The Talmud Yerushalmi explains that from midday onward was the time for the offering of the *korban Pesach*—the paschal lamb, for the entire Jewish people. This was considered a Yom Tov for every person. The day a person offered his sacrifice was his Yom Tov, his holiday. Since it was considered a Yom Tov, it was therefore forbidden to do *melachah* ("work") that is usually prohibited for Yom Tov. Rabbeinu Asher (the Rash) explains that "...therefore, even in today's time, without the Temple being here and without the offering of the actual *korban Pesach*, the Yom Tov component has not dissolved. From midday of Erev Pesach onward, we should not do any *melachah*. Furthermore, the Rabbeinu Nissim (the Ran) in *Pesachim* states, "Something that became forbidden through a vote of the *Chachamim* ("Sages") does not become permissible even if the original reason they forbade it no longer applies! When they said it was forbidden to work after *chatzos* on Erev Pesach, it was mandated for the entire Jewish people—even those who dwell in *chutz la'aretz*—outside of Israel." The reason is that it was once a holiday that had been established for the entire Jewish people. Reb Yechiel Michel Epstein, in his halachic work *Aruch Hashulchan, paskens* that someone who does *melachah* after *chatzos* on Erev Pesach will not only fail to see a blessing from his efforts, he will actually be cursed.

How often in life do we meet people who feel that they can do things differently than the rest of society. It is complete arrogance even to perform mitzvos when they are clearly being done outside the normative Halachah. What gives an individual the right to decide that, in *his* opinion, he thinks the law, the *halachah*, should be such and such, or he feels the law should be in accordance with so and so, even though there is an accepted approach according to the *Shulchan Aruch*. Even if there is an opinion that supports this outside practice, it is nevertheless a sign of haughtiness and will not last.

Community is wonderful. It provides friends, warmth, help, encouragement, and so much more. It also provides guidelines. Trust Am Yisrael. There is great wisdom in our people and our customs. Let us align ourselves with the norm—following normative Halachah and Jewish practice.

REGARDLESS OF WHETHER THE
GROWTH IS BENIGN OR POSITIVE, WE
MUST MAINTAIN A HEALTHY OUTLOOK
FOR MEANINGFUL GROWTH WITHIN
OURSELVES.

CHAPTER SEVEN

GROWTH

W hy was the Torah given in the desert?
One famous idea advanced by *Chazal* appears in *Bamidbar Rabbah* 1:7. The Torah was given with three things: fire, water, and earth. These three things are accessed for free by anyone in the world; so too the words of the Torah are also for free. Furthermore, anyone who does not make himself like a desert and ownerless will not be able to acquire the wisdom of the Torah. In other words, the desert is a place which is *hefker* ("ownerless") and therefore, anyone has a right to the Torah. I would like to suggest an alternative reason why the Torah was given and, more importantly, received in the desert.

The Book of *Bamidbar* descriptively illustrates the places in the desert the Jewish people traveled through for forty years. Wandering in the desert for forty years was the punishment the Jews incurred as a result of the episode of the spies. The straw that broke the camel's back was the *lashon hara* the spies spoke about Eretz Yisrael. This offense was compounded by the vast majority of Jews believing it. But, prior to this, the Jewish people swayed back and forth between good and bad. They received the Torah, but then went almost immediately to the sin of the Golden Calf. The generation of the desert was known as the *dor de'ah*—the generation of knowledge—who traveled from the lowest levels of Egypt as slaves up to the crown of accepting the

Torah. In a generation that was nourished by the manna from Heaven and the water from Miriam's well, there still remained an element of people who complained and wanted to go back to Egypt. It took forty years for the Jews to perfect themselves and merit going into the land of Israel.

Think about the desert.

As difficult as it is to traverse desert terrain, there are some upsides in comparison to paved roads. Paved roads, unlike "roads" of sand, have potholes, caused by fatigue of the road surface. Once a pothole forms, it grows through continued stress on the cracks. Potholes can grow to several feet in width causing serious road accidents.

Sand, on the other hand, fills the void made by something else that removed it. The terrain of the desert always remains the same; heat or cold has no effect on it. The message given to us is that the Torah is our guide for traveling in the desert.

Life is a journey that takes us in many different directions—some good and others not. Some of the roads we choose to take are at times laden with "potholes," potentially dangerous for our spiritual wellbeing. Hitting a spiritual pothole will throw off our personal alignment, rattling our inner equilibrium, making it more difficult for us to get to our destination. Unfortunately, the damage sustained from hitting spiritual potholes may go undetected, leaving latent damage. While sand may be difficult to traverse, there are not any bumps which can create serious inner damage.

Life is full of potholes; we must be aware of them and know how to navigate around them. If, by chance, we do hit a pothole, we need to consciously work to get back on track. Certain challenges come up in life, throwing us off our good daily routines of davening, learning, doing *chesed*, and so forth. Potholes jar us and alert us to quickly seek out the smooth surface of the road. On the other hand, driving through sand, although it may be arduous at times, if we slow down then we can avoid those devastating bumps.

The Torah is the navigation system for the Jewish people. The system must be checked and serviced all the time. If things go unchecked after a major bump in life, then other parts of the system will begin to go bad. If a person was doing a mitzvah consistently and by accident did not do it one time, then he must reset the system right away, otherwise, other mitzvos will begin to be affected.

The potholes of life are inevitable; we will all, at times, hit a pothole. Just as we may inadvertently hit a pothole while driving on our modern roads and will check for any resulting damage which may have been done to our car, even more so must we recognize the need to examine possible spiritual potholes, and, when detected, endeavor to make the necessary repairs.

◆ ◆ ◆

Language and speech can be very tricky at times. Sometimes we say something and do not realize or appreciate what we have actually said. On the other hand, there are times when words that come from our lips are pure gems, giving deep meaning to the simple vocabulary we have used. And finally, there are those rare times when we may make a statement which somehow is profound, expressing wisdom that we did not know we possessed!

A common occurrence that we have all been faced with is standing and waiting for the elevator. If we are standing on a floor other than the bottom or top one, there will usually be two buttons nearby to choose from. Presumably, we push the top button if our intention is to go to a higher floor and the bottom button if we want to reach a lower floor. However, it is irrelevant which button you push if someone already riding in the elevator made a contrary choice. For example, if you were on the fifth floor and wanted to go to the second floor, you probably would push the bottom button. If the elevator has someone in it and is already going to the eighth floor, then the elevator will go up to the eighth floor and then come back down to get you on the fifth floor and continue to the second. Nevertheless, when the person is going to the eighth floor, the elevator will stop on the fifth, the doors will open, and you probably will ask who's inside, "Going down?" And the person will answer, "No. Sorry, it's going up!"

People also go up and down. Some individuals and families grow while others...

When the Torah relates that Moshe's father, Amram, went out from the house of Levi and married Yocheved, it states: *"Va'yeilech ish mi'beis Levi."* The word *va'yeilech* ("and he went") will become synonymous with Moshe, as he was the product of this union. It is the symbol for Moshe; he will never just stand around, he will always be on the go. He forever had a desire and a thirst to raise himself spiritually to higher levels. The Ramban explains that Moshe went to each and every member of Klal Yisrael to inform them of his departure from the world and that they should not worry upon his death. This, the Ramban says, is also part of *holeich*: he is *going* to help raise the spirits of his fellow Jews. According to some opinions, there was nowhere else for Moshe to go, and therefore it was time for HaShem to call him up to *Shamayim*.

Moshe's entire life was trying to climb the ladder of spirituality in order to get closer to God. Part of his own personal growth is attributed to his caring for and working for the Jewish people. He was never satisfied with the current level of the Jewish people's relationship to HaShem and with his own spiritual quest. His life was centered upon climbing higher and higher. One of the most fundamental questions we can ask ourselves is whether we are going up or down. Are we in better or worse spiritual shape than we were a year ago? We must ask the honest and difficult questions: Do we *want* to be going up or could we not care less and just plunge down?

We must ask ourselves, *Why am I investing so much money and time for Jewish education, kosher food, and other mitzvos if I truly do not care about going down?*

Think about directions in life the next time you are on an elevator and it stops at a floor and someone asks you, "Going up or going down?" Our spiritual lives have ups and downs. Are we pushing the correct buttons in order to go in the right direction? Sometimes we need to get out of one elevator if it's broken or stuck in one place and use an alternative method in order to keep pushing ourselves upward.

Think about it: Where are we going?

◆ ◆ ◆

The subtle messages we give to toddlers and tots are more powerful and influential than we realize. Basic staples in a child's toy repertoire are blocks and Lego pieces. From the very early stages of life, we teach by demonstrating the importance of a good solid foundation. Typically, children enjoy building something tall and then having it topple over. For the young child, the joy is in the rebuilding, toppling down, and rebuilding again. The challenge is teaching a child how to build for fun, which is only temporary, and then graduate to constructing something that is permanent, something which hopefully will not fall down over the course of a lifetime. Another and perhaps greater lesson for a child or adolescent to grapple with as he matures in his thinking is that sometimes cracks form within the walls, or the bricks on top become loose, and he needs to develop strategies to ensure that the wall will not collapse.

I am a firm (no pun intended) believer that cracks in a wall will always be there and rickety bricks will always threaten to fall down. The strengthening of the foundation which holds up the wall should be considered more important than directly fixing the cracks or the rickety bricks on top. Solidifying the foundation will ultimately prevent those cracks from appearing in the first place. Fixing the cracks or gluing the top loose bricks is more of a Band-Aid solution to a problem that will return over time. Fixing the problem requires going back to those original building blocks and strengthening the core values and issues at hand. This may be challenged in the contemporary building of physical structures, but in spiritual matters the *yesod*—the foundation—is where it all lies.

A model class I gave to fourth graders early on in my career was quite memorable. The section being taught addressed Yaakov Avinu waking up after his dream about the angels going up and down the ladder. In the morning, Yaakov awakened and, upon realizing the holiness of that spot, poured oil over a *matzeivah*—a slab of stone—and consecrated it. During the class, I focused on the *shorashim* ("roots") of the words. After the class, one of the observers asked me what the root of *matzevah* is. I knew it was not *matzav* and told him that I did not know. He appreciated my honesty and went on to tell me it is *nitzav*—standing.

I look back now and realize that the stone which Yaakov set up was not only a physical slab of stone; it was the bedrock upon which the foundations of Judaism would be established. Most commentaries describe the holiness of the place as being the site of the Beis HaMikdash and the area of lighting the Menorah. In addition to the physical place being holy, the message of building a wall represents a distinction and separation between the Jewish people—following the Torah and all its laws—and the outside gentile world, which is sometimes diametrically opposite to many of the principles of the Torah.

The highlight of *korbanos* is the reciting of the *Tamid*—the daily offering. The reason for saying the daily offering is taught in two places in *Shas, Taanis* 27b and *Megillah* 31b. The Gemara states that Avraham Avinu said to HaShem, "Maybe the Jewish people are going to sin and be destroyed like the generation of the Flood and be wiped out." God assured Avraham that would not happen. Avraham asked, "How will I know that to be true?" God told Avraham to take a calf and offer it as a sacrifice, assuring Avraham "so too your children will do the same." Avraham responded that may all be well in the times when we have a Temple to offer sacrifices, but at a time that there is no Beis HaMikdash, what will they do? HaShem answered Avraham, "*I have already established for them the order of korbanos ("sacrifices"), that as long as they recite them verbally, I will credit them as if they brought the actual animal sacrifice, and I will forgive all of their sins.*"

The *Anshei Knesses HaGedolah*—the Men of the Great Assembly—established and formulated the prayer service for us in place of sacrifices. Like every structure that is built with a strong foundation at the bottom, so too the "building" of davening every morning and afternoon begins with *korbanos*. When davening, a person must build up from the foundation and therefore must recite *korbanos*. Otherwise *Pesukei D'Zimra*, the next section of prayer, does not have something to support it. It is imperative that we come on time to services and daven in the correct sequence if we want our prayers to be solid and successful.

People—individuals and communities alike—are built upon foundations which are hopefully strong. Shuls, schools, and other institutions build structures in their part of the Jewish community— some strong, others weak. As time passes, new buildings are constructed while others come down. There is always a change in the landscape of a community; sometimes the walls begin to show cracks, and some of the stones become loose. What should we each do when we feel threatened by weakened surroundings, by unstable walls? What do we do when our own personal "building" is challenged and threatens to fall apart?

The best approach is to reinforce the solid foundation with which we started. Each of us knows what made us strong in the beginning. What is the substance of our foundation? How was it laid? Was it from deep commitment to Shabbos observance, kashrus, family purity, doing acts of *chesed*, learning, davening, focusing on our children's Jewish education, and so forth? When our own walls or the walls of our community begin to show cracks, we need to revisit the element that sparked every one of us and reinforce our own, as well as the community's, foundations. We must realize that the best offense is a good defense. We cannot always fix something that belongs to someone else, but we can always fix ourselves and work together to repair or rebuild an area of weakness within our community.

Our ways will always remain strong as long as we return and strengthen the core elements of what propelled us here in the first place...the foundation of the Torah.

◆ ◆ ◆

Vehicle Code Section 22400: No person shall drive upon a highway at such a slow speed as to impede or block the normal and reasonable movement of traffic unless the reduced speed is necessary for safe operation, because of a grade, or in compliance with law.

Vehicle Code Section 23582 and basic speed law 22350: No person shall drive a vehicle upon a highway at a speed greater than is reasonable or prudent, having due regard for weather, visibility, the traffic on, and the surface and width of, the highway, and in no event at a speed which endangers the safety of persons or property.

These California laws do not only apply to driving, but, in theory, apply wherever we are the driving force behind something. One of the many challenges that face a pulpit rabbi is maintaining a good speed for davening. On a recent trip to the East Coast, I found myself davening in a number of different places, some fast, some slow. In one place, the rabbi took longer than usual to finish Shema. I looked around and noticed how the attendees were becoming disengaged from the service due to this lull in the davening. In another shul, the rabbi finished his Shemoneh Esrei relatively quickly and, as the davening proceeded, left behind a majority of the *mispallelim* ("worshippers").

We are also the drivers of our family's destiny. The leader of a group, be it a shul, school, yeshivah, or especially a home, must maintain the necessary equilibrium for traveling the road of life. One must work diligently to create a balance for every individual, student, and child. This requires patience and vision to recognize where each person is, where he or she has to get to and how to get there. Going too fast can easily make the individual fall behind in the program, thereby creating a feeling of isolation or frustration. On the other hand, going too slowly can create a sense of boredom and a lack of challenge for the person, leading him to find other things—good or bad—to occupy his time and space.

A primary and essential ingredient to maintaining this delicate balancing act is to establish a consistent firmness of the physical and spiritual needs of the family and institution. Too often, if there is an imbalance one way or the other, there is a complete breakdown of the structure. Human beings are comprised of both *guf* and *neshamah*—the body and the soul—and, therefore, require each to nurture the other. This concept was brought out by Reb Meir Shapiro, the Rav of Lublin.

At the end of *Sefer Bereishis*, Yosef bestows a blessing of sorts upon his brothers. In *Bereishis* 50:24, the Torah states: "*Vayomer Yosef el echav, Anochi meis, ve'Elokim pakod yifkod eschem v'he'elah eschem min ha'aretz asher nishba l'Avraham, Yitzchak, u'l'Yaakov—Yosef said to his brothers, 'I*

am about to die, but God will surely remember you and bring you up out of *this land to the land that He swore to Avraham, Yitzchak, and Yaakov.'* "
Rav Meir Shapiro explains the double wording of *"pakod yifkod—surely* *remember"*—as a sign that Yosef gave to his brothers. He was saying that there is no true *geulah* ("redemption") for the Jewish people without the tidings being given over in a double, repeated action. What is the significance of the double terminology? Throughout history, when the Jewish people are redeemed from their exile, it is through both spirituality and physicality. The warning is that there is no true redemption if it is only on the physical side without the spiritual side; this is a false hope. For example, if we were to hear that we could return to Eretz Yisrael, but could not live a life based upon Torah, then we would know that this is a false redemption. The only true redemption must come in the form of a physical *and* spiritual salvation. Another example of this is found in *Midrash Seichel Tov*, on the *pasuk Shemos* 3:16, where Moshe says: *"Pakod pakadeti eschem—I have surely remembered you."* Immediately thereafter, the Jewish people responded in the affirmative. Why? Because they heard about the salvation in the doubled verbiage.

Rav Meir Simcha of Dvinsk, in his commentary *Meshech Chochmah*, explains the double wording as a message that only comes from a *Navi* ("Prophet"). Only when a *Navi* uses the double language should we, the Jewish people, act upon his words. If it does not conform to this guideline, then a person or people should not act upon the redemption and go up to Israel. The words of redemption must mimic the message of Moshe Rabbeinu and Yosef before him—that the Jewish people will be remembered and redeemed to go up and return to Eretz Yisrael. Only these words of salvation and redemption can direct us to going back up to Eretz Yisrael, unlike the story where the Bnei Ephraim went up on their own accord without receiving the message and the blessing of redemption from an authorized person (*Bamidbar* 14:40–45).

As we drive along the roadways, we see signs that give us direction. There are manuals and guidebooks that teach the laws of driving, safety, mechanics, and the overall responsibility of driving. So, too, in our driving through life we must study the handbook. The handbook contains rules, laws, regulations, punishments, and rewards. The Torah is the handbook of life, given to us to guide us through every one of life's situations. There are signs that are shown to us and there are people to turn to for directions. We all need to consult with teachers and rabbis who can help monitor each person's pace in his or her personal path toward greater spirituality.

A balancing act is one which requires perseverance, dedication, concentration, and direction. This is no easy feat, but we will succeed if we have the proper tools at our disposal. A Torah community surrounded by schools and a shul gives each of us and our families the ability to balance this act. Teachers, rabbis, and the guidelines of the Torah are there for the taking. Do not get caught speeding or moving at such a slow pace as to block normal and reasonable growth!

◆　◆　◆

Do we demand as much of ourselves as we do from others?

People have high expectations from coworkers, friends, rabbis, teachers, principals, and people with whom they interact. Quite often we are disappointed with the level of perceived commitment and service that we receive. This is driven by the fact that we reason to ourselves that we could have and, unquestionably, would have done it better. We must always make an honest evaluation of our own situation and take a hard look before making such a judgment. Would we *really* do better under those same circumstances? What is our vision for providing successful management skills? Do we currently serve people based upon need in each specific, unique situation?

I believe people would consider a business to be successful if it accomplished many of the following goals:

- Loyal and dedicated to client needs
- Willing to go above and beyond in order to meet customer expectations
- Maximizing the existing human resources in the business

- Knowledgeable about current labor legislation, law, and best practices

- Result-oriented

Very often, business personnel fulfill most of these goals, but unfortunately customers today do not have the patience to wait for the results of their efforts. People erroneously interpret a lack of immediate resolution to be the result of inefficiency, ineptitude, or a lack of customer service. Unfortunately, customers typically do not see or even care about the big picture or taking other possible considerations into account, choosing instead to only think about their own best interests. For example, a person may be waiting in line for service and, while becoming increasingly irate for not receiving the desired assistance in a timely manner, begin complaining loudly even though the clerk was attending to an emergency that had higher priority. We do not know why things are delayed, but most often we should exercise understanding, because unbeknown to us, there might be something more urgent going on. Unfortunately, as much as we believe we are patient and reasonable, that is not always the case. When the shoe is on the other foot, we want people to understand when *we* are not as efficient as they expect us to be, and we are disappointed at the criticisms that might come our way, yet we tend to be just as unreasonable and impatient when it is our turn to be sympathetic.

There is an old joke about a Jew who wants to learn to have patience, but he wants to learn it right now! This is not a new phenomenon, as the Torah records (*Shemos* 32:1): "*The nation saw that Moshe was delayed in coming down from the mountain. They became agitated and gathered around Aharon and said, 'Arise. Make us a god who will walk before us, because this man Moshe, who took us out from Egypt, we don't know where he is.'*"

According to the Maharil Diskin, Rav Yehoshua Leib Diskin, there are many different opinions among the Rabbis regarding whether the Jews actually wanted to worship an idol or simply to construct a figure to replace Moshe Rabbeinu. It is difficult to determine the mindset of the Jewish people at that point in our development. Therefore, since we know a Jew must always give the benefit of the doubt, then how much more so, to give the benefit of the doubt to the entire nation that they had no intention of wanting to serve an idol. Nevertheless, we see a pattern of succumbing to impatience with the Jewish people. Not long after witnessing the awesome deeds of HaShem when He freed the Jews from Egypt, there was an expressed desire to turn back: work and food were available in Egypt. Another example followed after they experienced walking through the Sea of Reeds, feeling the power of God's Presence as they were miraculously saved while the advancing Egyptians were drowned. Soon after they had reached dry land, they actually asked: "*Is God among us...or not*" (*Shemos* 17:7). Also by the Golden Calf, despite the fact that through every crisis Moshe was there for the Jewish people, they were still not able to demonstrate patience.

Things have not changed as much as we think over the past few thousand years! We are as impatient and demanding as ever. Sometimes we can find ourselves not sure whether God is listening or is just not providing the "customer service" that we anticipate. Obstinately, we might foolishly think: "I mean, c'mon, I pray, I learn, I do a few good deeds here and there, and yet I do not get what I want, when I want it!"

If we really analyze it, the *client* services that we receive from HaShem are truly incredible. We do not realize it, but here is a sample of the infinite list that God offers us:

- 24/7/365 total availability for any reason (and, of course, for all emergencies)
- Quick response to fill last minute orders
- Caring, compassionate, and merciful, as the situation requires

Even after the greatest national committed sin, the Sin of the Golden Calf, HaShem (answering Moshe's plea) was, is, and always will be there for the Jewish people. In summary, HaShem's treatment of us—his favorite and best client—includes, but is not limited to, demonstrating: His reliability, dedication, commitment, passion, safety, and pledge to protect the Jewish people. We need to cut God a little slack. We may not be able to see or understand the larger picture, but we can be assured that for HaShem that picture is in clear view. The Jewish people made a six-hour mistake in their calculations regarding Moshe's return. That mistake cost us a lot in the development of our nation. Our tendency to want to see our needs met instantly has to be kept in check. There really is a grand plan; it is our obligation to understand that and to put our personal desires into perspective.

Today, *baruch HaShem*, we look back at our long history and can see that HaShem has us in mind. The "customer service" is there. Let it be on His terms and not on our demands, otherwise we risk another kind of episode like the sin of the Golden Calf, Heaven forbid. Rather, we need to reflect on the lessons of our long and miraculous history. Just as during the time of *Megillas Esther*, when things looked very bleak and HaShem was there to save us, so too today, in these turbulent, difficult times, HaShem is here to guide and help us.

He gives us so much. What can we give Him back?

◆ ◆ ◆

The Rambam, in his *sefer Moreh Nevuchim*, writes that one of the reasons HaShem commanded us to bring sacrifices was in order to distance ourselves from foreign worship, from idolatry. He explains that the Jews lived in Egypt, Ur Casdim (now considered part of modern Iraq), and India (since 562 B.C.E.), where the culture was to worship these very same animals that we offered as sacrifices. It is for this very reason that we specifically offered cows, sheep, and goats: they were viewed as gods and were worshiped in the very countries where we lived.

The Ramban explains the reason for animal sacrifices was for a *rei'ach nicho'ach LaHaShem*—a pleasing fragrance for HaShem. It is important to understand that the sole purpose of the sacrifices was to bringing offerings to HaShem because HaShem is the only one we serve. The Ramban writes that the word *korban* expresses a term of "closeness" and oneness. The *Meshech Chochmah*, in quoting the Ramban, says that the offering of animal sacrifices was to cause all the nations of the world to get close to HaShem. Whichever opinion we choose, the common denominator is for us to demonstrate our connection to HaShem.

Sefer Vayikra focuses on animal sacrifices that are brought onto the Altar for a host of different purposes. Whether the sacrifice is offered as a sin-offering, a thanksgiving, an elevation, a guilt, a doubt, or a daily sacrifice, they all have at least one thing in common: the animal must be blemish-free.

I would like to share a personal insight as to why a blemish-free animal is necessary to achieve the purpose of any sacrifice. Keep in mind that God does not need our animals or our sacrifices; rather, the sacrifice is provided for us to use as a means of communication and connection to HaShem.

The sacrifices are, in actuality, offered in place of ourselves; we should be offering up ourselves as a sacrificial offering for our wrongdoing. Instead, Hashem lets us use an animal in our place, which are thrown upon the Altar. HaShem commands us that the animals are here in this world to serve us[4] and that they should be our representatives in the performance of this mitzvah. The Bartenura writes that the world is sustained because of our service to HaShem, and that service is primarily the *korbanos*—the sacrifices—that we bring. But, again, why does the animal have to be blemish-free?

Having a *mum* ("a blemish"), by nature, is very human. No two people are created the same; therefore, a deficiency in one person will not be found to be exactly the same in another person, and vice versa. HaShem created us with the specific goal of working consistently to perfect ourselves, knowing full well that human beings are *not* perfect. Therefore, as a result of our actions, we bring a sacrifice to emulate what we strive to be: perfect. Since we are not perfect, we simulate the concept of perfection through an animal which is totally free of any physical blemishes. The message of blemish-free is for us to recognize our own imperfections.

If a person thinks he is perfect, then he will not be able to get close to God. Knowing our weaknesses gives us the ability to work harder to correct our ways. Knowing that we are deficient and lacking in certain areas gives us the push to serve HaShem more diligently and to more

---

4   *Kli Yakar, Vayikra.*

sincerely ask Him to help us. A person who does not recognize his shortcomings will never grow, and ultimately that person will come crashing down; his very conceit, his inability to recognize the weak underpinnings in his life, will be the cause of his own ruin. The person who exudes an attitude of superiority, of being better than others, is in actuality stating that he and his kind or his friends are perfect, and that you, on the other hand, are not—you are flawed, less intelligent, and less capable. Such a person is saying that he and those close to him do not have to grow spiritually because they have maxed out; there is no reason or room to grow any more.

Perfection is not part of G-d's expectation for us. Only G-d is perfect. We, on the other hand, are mortal, and, being human, we each need to acknowledge and try to understand our specific limitations and to work throughout our lives to improve ourselves.

Through the bringing of *korbanos*, however, we are openly trying to attain a state of being blemish-free, but we are not claiming that we are blemish-free. People who point out deficiencies and inadequacies in others are exhibiting a form of *gaavah* ("haughtiness"). *Chazal* tell us that *gaavah* is a form of idolatry. Possibly the reason they equate haughtiness with idolatry is because those who look at themselves as superior to others, who view others in terms of their foibles and weaknesses, become increasingly more enamored with themselves and actually become deluded into thinking they are truly blemish-free— that they have no need to bring sacrifices because there is nothing about them to correct. Feeling they are perfect in a sense equates them to being godlike. Only an imperfect individual needs to reach out to HaShem; the haughty feel no need for this. They put themselves on the level of HaShem, never needing to correct anything; it's only others who need God.

Unfortunately, in our days we live without the Beis HaMikdash. We do not have the opportunity to offer animal sacrifices as our ancestors did. The Rabbis, of blessed memory, constructed *tefillah* ("prayer") in place of the sacrifices. Davening and prayer is the modern way of getting close to HaShem. Through our davening, we can apologize and recognize our mistakes, faults, and deficiencies. This is a tool specifically designed to get close to HaShem. The person who acts in a haughty manner is doomed to live an unfulfilling and empty life, a life devoid of any substance or meaning. The classic *mussar sefer Orchos Tzaddikim* discusses *gaavah*/haughtiness in the very first chapter. The author declares that haughtiness brings a person to desire, and it is one of three things that destroys a person's life, as recorded by one of the great *Tannaim*. Rabbi Elazar HaKapar, in *Pirkei Avos* 4:28, teaches us that "desire, honor, and haughtiness remove a person from the world." The *mishnah* uses the word "world," not defining it as this world or as the World to Come, but it is very likely referring to the removal of such a person from *both* worlds, *Olam HaZeh* and *Olam HaBa*—this world and the World to Come. Haughtiness, a need to seek and receive personal honor, the desire to prove superiority, in the view of *Chazal* actually causes such an individual to lose his share both here and in the next world. He acts as if he is a god—an open form of idolatry. Such a person cannot get close to HaShem. This world in which he currently lives will eventually crash around him. Unfortunately, tragically, we have all witnessed this scenario.

Rav Eliyahu Lopian, *zt"l*, in his work *Lev Eliyahu*, comments on a telling point in the verse (*Bamidbar* 12:11) in which Aharon says to Moshe: "*Al na sasheis aleinu chatas asher noalnu va'asher chatanu—I beg you, do not cast a sin upon us, for we have been foolish and we have sinned.*" He states that HaShem was angry at us for not admitting our mistakes immediately. David Hamelech, on the other hand, in the episode with Nasan HaNavi, immediately declares "*chatasi—I sinned.*" We need to admit our mistakes freely and readily. Admitting our mistakes and imperfections is a key to getting even closer to perfection.

The message written here is not limited to individuals alone. Schools, businesses, shuls, and even entire neighborhoods and communities, can be caught in the trap of haughtiness.

Let us view the message of the *korbanos* as an avenue to grow in a deep and meaningful way. Try using prayer as a means to get closer to the Creator, the One whom each of us needs every minute of our lives.

Finally, stop trying to show that you are better than others by putting others down. To do so, in reality, puts you down as an idol worshipper. Let us correct our ways to be able to offer the actual *korbanos* in the *Bayis Shelishi* ("third Beis HaMikdash") in Yerushalayim, speedily in our days.

❖ ❖ ❖

The Torah states (*Devarim* 30:15): *"Re'ei Nasati lefanecha ha'yom es ha'chaim v'es ha'tov v'es ha'maves v'es ha'ra—See—I have placed before you today life and good, and death and evil."* Rav Moshe Feinstein, of blessed memory, asks, "What does the word *ha'yom*—today—come to teach us?" He explains that every day a person has to choose between two paths that are in front of him. He points out that it doesn't make a difference whether a person has chosen the incorrect path up until this point and is now deciding to choose the good path. In fact, he says that even if the person has chosen the good path every day up until now, he should not come to rely on this for the future. We cannot think that since we have chosen the good path one time that we will automatically choose it the next time. Rather, a person must recalculate the situation and come to make the correct decision every time. Rav Moshe concludes by saying, "Every single day a person must know and recognize that there are two paths in front of him; each and every time he must conquer the *yetzer hara* and choose the path of HaShem to perform *tzedakah* and *mishpat*—kindness and righteousness."

Part of the tactic of the *yetzer hara* is to sometimes give in and let the person win a battle. Once someone has done the right thing, his guard might be lowered, so that the next time he faces a challenge, he feels overconfident that he will automatically make a good decision without thinking carefully about all of the ramifications that are entailed. Unfortunately, that is not the way it works. Every situation has to be reviewed deliberately and with care, as if it is the first time he is rendering such a decision.

The Torah mentioned good and evil but there are two other words which need to be addressed: right and wrong. As a rabbi, I commonly encounter individuals who are convinced that they are right...that they are *always* right...particularly in areas of *hashkafah* and interpersonal relations. Once a person thinks and knows he is right, he cannot even listen to the opposing side's argument and logic. There is a complete mental shutdown, making it difficult, even impossible, to discuss the flaws in that person's reasoning. He simply *knows* he is right.

Rav Moshe's understanding of the *pasuk* can be used not only for choosing between good and evil, but also for determining what is right and what is wrong. Determining right and wrong is a decision and choice that also must be made each time with careful deliberation. A person should start with an attitude of "I don't know" and proceed to investigate. A person should listen carefully to the advice of competent people, particularly the rabbis, as well as insightful family members or friends. No one can expect to reach the right decision on his own. No one is right all of the time.

◆ ◆ ◆

From time to time, I speak about some of my pet peeves. I ask those present if they want to hear all five hundred of my pet peeves or only the top ten! So...what are pet peeves? Pet peeves often involve specific behaviors or reactions (sometimes eccentric) that a person displays. We normally observe these pet peeves in ourselves, our spouses, our supervisors, etc. A key aspect of a pet peeve is that what unnerves one person may very well seem acceptable to others. For example, a supervisor may have a pet peeve about people leaving the copier lid raised, or react angrily or become annoyed when others interrupt his or her speaking, or be upset by the messy desks of subordinates. That same supervisor may witness employees coming to work late and not feel any annoyance whatsoever.

One of the top ten pet peeves I have concerns *heicha kedushah*. *Tefillas Minchah*—the afternoon prayer service—is relatively short. It consists of the Shemoneh Esrei and a few *tehillim* said before and after, concluding with Aleinu. In order to shorten the davening, *heicha kedushah* eliminates a full repetition of the Amidah. Instead of starting with the silent Amidah followed by a repetition, the *shaliach tzibbur* begins the Amidah out loud until *kedushah* and then everyone recites *kedushah* together. After *kedushah*, the chazzan continues the Amidah silently and the congregation will then say their silent Amidah as well. From where does this wording come? *Heicha* is the Litvish pronunciation of *hoiche*, which means "loud." Perhaps it means that the beginning of the *shaliach tzibbur*'s Amidah is said aloud by him so that we can answer Amen to his *berachah* of *kedushah*, which is one of the most important *berachos* that one should hear from *chazaras HaShatz*—the *shaliach tzibbur*'s repetition.

The *heicha kedushah* is brought down in Halachah as applicable in just two instances. The first instance is when reciting the entire repetition will impact the study of Torah—i.e., it will result in individuals having to cut down on some of their Torah learning. The second scenario is when it's very late in the day and the minyan might miss the cut-off time to finish saying the Minchah service. Keep in mind that the entire recitation of the Shemoneh Esrei could be said in about three minutes by someone who is fluent and fluid in reading Hebrew. Unfortunately, this (sometimes necessary) mechanism within Halachah has been abused and manipulated at times without any justification. *Heicha kedushah* is implemented at weddings, trips, and even sporting events.

When shortcuts are used, people lose out on the full benefits. One of the more famous quotes from my *rosh yeshivah*, Rav Berel Wein, was that "there are no shortcuts in life." It seems clear that he meant that if a person can cut through some steps in a process or get to a goal quicker, there is always a price to pay. The high price of *heicha kedushah* is that of missing out on saying Amen to all the *berachos* that we would have otherwise heard during the repetition. In establishing the *minhagim* of Beis Medrash Govoha in Lakewood, New Jersey, Rav Aharon Kotler implemented *heicha kedushah* for the yeshivah for the first reason mentioned above. An exception was made during Chanukah in order to recite the full repetition so that people would hear *Al HaNisim*, which falls under the guise of *pirsumei nisa*—making the miracle well known—a very important element of the holiday.

In *Bamidbar* 24:16, the Torah states: *"Neum shomeiah imrei Keil, v'yodeiah daas Elyon—The saying of him who hears the words of God, and knows the knowledge of the Most High."* Rashi explains that this knowing of the Most High is Bilaam, who knew the exact moment of God's anger during the day. The Gemara in *Berachos* 7a states: "No creature was able to know the exact moment God would get angry except for the wicked Bilaam." Rav Meir Chodosh was asked why was it that Moshe Rabbeinu did not know that exact moment and yet Bilaam knew?

Rav Meir Chodosh answered that Moshe Rabbeinu did not *want* to know this kind of information. He was not interested in knowing the exact moment that HaShem would be angry and therefore did not know it. But despite knowing when HaShem would be angry, an easy and quick way toward the Jews' downfall, Bilaam was unsuccessful in his attempt to utilize this knowledge for evil purposes. In fact, his only power was the knowledge itself, this exact moment, and it backfired on him. Moshe Rabbeinu, of course, did not want to know the time when HaShem would be angry. Moreover, he was not interested in shortcuts, in the quick fixes of life.

In Judaism, halachic leniencies are built into the system because the life of a Jew requires it. Judaism, through Halachah, allows that life is not always perfect and sometimes we must do mitzvos and obligations in a *b'dieved* or ex-post facto way and not only in the *l'chatchilah*, or preferred manner. These circumstances are not permitted to become the norm. We can only use an alternative method when the need arises; we are not permitted to use it just for the sake of convenience.

It is the performance of mitzvos that brings us closer to HaShem. The message we send to God when we use a shortcut is that we are more interested in doing the mundane, rather than getting closer to Him. We live with enough distractions that challenge us, sometimes actually hindering us from getting closer to HaShem. The *seder ha'yom* ("order of the day") is created for us to have fixed times and ways to remember HaShem and to connect. Cutting out or shortening these few mechanisms takes a toll on our relationship with the Almighty. Let's try to stick to the main road and not take any shortcuts, as they inevitably will take us further away from our ultimate destination. After all, in life there really are not any shortcuts.

◆ ◆ ◆

There is an old joke about a wife wanting to clean out the garage from the fifty-year accumulation of "stuff" collected throughout her marriage. Most of the things are in the garage for a very good reason... there is no longer any use for them. So the wife throws out the golf clubs that had not been used for years. When her husband finds out, he gets all upset, even though he never goes golfing anymore.

Of course, we all get attached to things and we feel we can never part from them. Old, broken, or even in the best condition, it does not matter. We feel the need to save it all because we may need at least some of it sometime in the future, or we think that it will increase in value with age and prove to be worth a great deal in the future. This is called the "packrat syndrome." Some people try to fight this off and have established a system by setting up rules as to whether or not an item gets tossed:

- Does the item have an actual use and will it get used?
- If the item were to get lost or if it were to break would it have to be replaced?
- Does the item have a designated place (as opposed to ending up in a junk drawer)?
- Is there a strong emotional attachment to the item?

If it does not fit these requirements, it needs to go into the trash or to be donated.

I am a quasi-packrat; I have this very same syndrome of holding onto items from my childhood or even from my children's younger years that will never be used again. I start to rationalize and convince myself that it definitely does fit one of the four criteria listed above and therefore I must save it.

Unfortunately, what people do not understand (myself included) is the fact that often we need to come to grips with how obsolete these items are in our lives. We used them in their correct time and place and now these items have no more use. It is much healthier for our own sake to rid ourselves of these things in order to move on in life. We need to leave our "baggage" behind, perhaps to shed the old in order to start over again for the future.

We find this same mentality in the Torah with regard to Pharaoh. In *Shemos* 13:17, Pharaoh sent out the Jews from Egypt as a result of the Ten Plagues. In fact, after the tenth plague, he was almost "throwing the Jews out," wanting to get rid of them because of what God did to his country. Only a few lines later, in 14:5, we read that it was told to Pharaoh that the Jews ran away! In the very same verse, it describes how once again Pharaoh had a change of heart, and he said, *"What have we done that we sent out the Jews from being slaves?"*

In reality, Pharaoh never intended to get rid of the Jewish people from his land. His intention was to let them go for a few days (put them in the garage) and eventually he would need them again. This crystalized when Pharaoh surveyed Egypt and saw the totality of its destruction from the plagues. He, and even the Egyptian army, realized that the country was decimated and that their only possession remaining was the Jews. The Egyptian agriculture, landscape, food chain, and economy were completely destroyed. But they still had difficulty "throwing out" what remained of their possessions, and therefore, even after agreeing to send the Jewish people out of Egypt, Pharaoh changed his heart once again. This time Pharaoh changed his heart and mind not due to the relief from a plague, but rather because the Jewish slaves were the only commodity remaining to Egypt.

The lesson that Pharaoh either did not know or refused to understand was that the Jewish people had to be in Egypt for a particular reason and for the specific amount of time of four hundred years. The time had come for us to leave and no longer be under the influence of Egypt; the Jewish people were blessed to have new "ownership" under the leadership of Moshe.

Spiritually speaking, we also carry baggage and old traits that we feel we cannot rid ourselves of. We say to ourselves, *How can I not do that anymore or how can I possibly start to do something now in my life that I have never done before?* If there is a fear or hesitancy or anxiety about getting rid of a bad character trait or taking on a new mitzvah, we should let go of that which is holding us back from growing in our service to HaShem. To let go of our old attitudes and conduct requires us to be open to venturing out of our comfort zone. At that point, we can see the world in a light that is open to beneficial change and growth.

◆ ◆ ◆

In life we often say "should've, would've, could've," or "shoulda, woulda, coulda," which really means "if I had it to do over again, this is the way I would do it." Unfortunately, we do not get to do things over again. There is no Undo button in the game of life; it is a one-way street upon which we are riding without even the ability to slow down or pause. We must make decisions, sometimes split-second choices, all the while continuing to roll along. One of the major challenges and possibly a life game-changer is to find a way to stop or slow down as much as possible in order to calculate the next move or decision we make in life for ourselves, for our families, or for our people.

After much "encouragement," Pharaoh finally "allowed" the Jewish people to leave Egypt. Think for a moment. What in the world was going on in Pharaoh's mind throughout the Ten Plagues?! After witnessing the total decimation of his country, one would think he would say, *Maybe I should have let the Jews go out earlier in order to spare me and my people some grief and loss.* To add insult to injury, after realizing that the Jews had left on a permanent journey, he hurriedly called up his army and chariots to chase them down, only to be devoured by the raging sea.

Some questions remain: When Pharaoh returned to Egypt after this final blow, did he experience any regret? Did he say he should have let the Jews go earlier? Did he consider that had he let them go earlier, he would have been better off?

The Torah states: *"Va'yehi b'shalach Paroh es ha'am v'lo nacham Elokim derech eretz plishtim ki karov hu ki amar Elokim pen yinacheim ha'am birosam milchamah v'shavu Mitzraimah—And it happened when Pharaoh sent the people out that God did not lead them by the way of the land of the Philistines, because it was near, for God said, 'Perhaps the people will reconsider when they see a war, and they will return to Egypt.'"* A famous rule repeated throughout Jewish commentary is that the word *va'yehi* implies that something bad is going to happen. In this instance, most commentators explain that *va'yehi* applies to the Jews. But perhaps it can be suggested that *va'yehi* relates to Pharaoh's ultimate demise that awaited him after the Jews reached the other side of the Sea of Reeds. What was it that gave Pharaoh pause to consider bringing the Jews back to Egypt and perhaps subject himself to more pain and suffering?

The answer lies in the fact that Pharaoh thought, *Maybe, just maybe, this time will be different.* Pharaoh read into the mindset of the Jews. In *Shemos* 14:15, as the Jews were backed up against the sea, they complained to Moshe. At that point HaShem said to Moshe: *"Why do you cry out to Me? Speak to the Children of Israel and let them journey!"* The Maharal teaches that the phrase used by HaShem "why do you cry out" tells us that they should not have cried. How could they *not* cry out at a time like this? The *Mechilta* brings two opinions regarding how the Jews should have handled this situation. They were backed up against the water and the Egyptian army was closing in on them. Rabbi Yehoshua says that their only option was to continue traveling forward into the water. Rabbi Eliezer says HaShem said to them, "My children, you are in a desperate situation and you are calling out for mercy?"

Rabbi Yehoshua explains this verse as follows: After all the Jewish people witnessed and experienced, seeing firsthand the Cloud of Glory and the Pillar of Fire lead them on their way, they had no need to cry out. According to Rabbi Eliezer: They should not have asked for mercy at this point; they should have made the following logical deduction. HaShem made dry land for one individual—Adam HaRishon. Just as HaShem said *"yikavu ha'mayim*—let the waters be gathered" and dry land appeared during Creation, how much more so now HaShem would gather the waters and dry up the land in order to allow an entire holy congregation safe passage!

The Maharal further explains that the natural way of the world is that water should cover land. Despite the fact that water naturally covers the land, HaShem had to go beyond nature and create a dry piece of land for Adam to inhabit. So too, HaShem went above nature to provide Klal Yisrael dry land to walk over. It is obvious that man needed dry land in order to survive on this earth. When the Jews left Egypt, the only way they could become a nation was *"ha'avaras ha'yam*—passing over the water." Because of this "passing over," we were called *Ivrim*. In a similar vein, Avraham was called an *Ivri* because he "passed over" from the other side of the river from Bavel to Eretz Yisrael in the physical sense and from the other side of religion in the spiritual sense. So too, Avraham's descendants passed over the dry land with *emunah* and *bitachon*, with "faith and trust" in God to save them. This is the *middah* ("character trait") that Avraham transmitted and which later became embodied in his children.

This "crossing" the barrier of faith and trust was the final blow to Pharaoh, causing him to finally give up. It was not until these final moments when the Jewish people actually reached the "other side" that Pharaoh realized his defeat and that there was no return. Until that actual crossing over occurred, Pharaoh was confident that he could recapture the Jews and bring them back to Egypt. Pharaoh should have recognized how much he lost and should have cut ties much earlier in the game.

Each and every one of us should learn a lesson from this idea. We need to know when to cut our losses. We all make mistakes in life; instead of trying to fix them, it may be better just to move on and start anew. Most times it is difficult to play catch-up; we would be better off just making a fresh start. It was critical that Nachshon ben Aminadav led the Jewish people forward by jumping into the sea, thereby not allowing the Jews to turn back toward Egypt so that they could "try to work it out." The Jewish people had faith as they crossed over the physical land, but the psychological barrier which faced them as they came to the Sea of Reeds was enormous. But nonetheless, they moved forward and did not look back.

The difference between Am Yisrael and the other nations of the world is that we continuously look forward. If we were constantly looking back on our history, we would become depressed. Rather, we look forward to the ultimate *geulah*. The lessons taught by Klal Yisrael should be adopted by its individual members who make up the group. Individually, we should look forward to a brighter future and cut the losses of our past performances.

◆ ◆ ◆

After three years of mouth discomfort, brace tightening, and not being able to bite into apples, my son's braces were finally removed. He immediately felt the freedom of his teeth and tongue. This was short-lived, however, as the orthodontist required that a retainer be worn all day for at least a year. The importance of the retainer cannot be underestimated, and my son was warned that if he did not wear the retainer, he would run the risk of his teeth shifting, thereby losing all that he had gained during the three years of wearing braces.

It takes a few years for something that was forcibly changed to stay in its new place permanently. We find this to be true in many other areas of life.

In today's world, there is an ever increasing focus on immediate weight loss, but unfortunately not on permanent weight loss. Millions of dollars are spent annually on dieting, exercising, and monitoring food consumption, but the results are most often lost, and the dieter reverts back to his previous weight. Sadly, it's not uncommon for the dieter to regain all of the previously lost weight and to gain even more weight than had been lost.

A report in the *New England Journal of Medicine*, dated October 27, 2011, examined why people typically gained back all of the weight that they lost. The article, entitled "Long-Term Persistence of Hormonal Adaptations to Weight Loss," focused on the changes that occur in hormones involved in the regulation of body weight. It was found that during the study, there was a significant increase in the subjects' appetite—and hunger. The conclusion of the study stated: "One year after initial weight reduction, levels of the circulating mediators of appetite that encourage weight regain after diet-induced weight loss do not revert to the levels recorded before weight loss. Long-term strategies to counteract this change may be needed to prevent obesity relapse." Dr. Stephen Bloom, an obesity researcher at Hammersmith Hospital in London, said the study needed to be repeated under more rigorous conditions, but added, "It is showing something I believe in deeply—it is very hard to lose weight." And the reason, he said, is that "your hormones work against you."

Spiritual hormones are the work of the *yetzer hara*—the Satan. Anyone who makes a commitment to change his way of religious life needs to do so over a long period of time. A commitment of this depth and complexity requires long-term, consistent focus and determination. When a person takes on a commitment to do a particular mitzvah or act, he must do it continuously for a few years in order to affect permanent change. Most often, individuals will state that they are going to change and actually do manage to accomplish this adaptation for a while, but for the change to be deep and permanent, the conscientious act of creating this change must take place over a period of at least a few years in order to make it an intrinsic part of the individual's new spiritual core makeup.

In the Torah, we learn a similar concept—permanent change takes a long time. In *Bereishis* 8:7, the Torah states: *"Va'yishalach es ha'oreiv, va'yeitzei va'yatzo va'shov ad yevoshes ha'mayim me'al ha'aretz."* Forty days after the Flood waters began to recede, Noach opened up the window and sent out the raven, and it flew out around the ark and came back. Later, Noach sent out the dove to see if the waters had receded from the earth. Rav Yehuda Mintz (1415–1508), in his *derashos*, writes that God showed other great miracles during the *Mabul* ("Flood"). For an entire year, the constellations, stars, moon, and sun stopped functioning. This was a miracle for the people in the *teivah* ("ark"), because the existence of mankind on Earth is dependent on the revolving solar system. Because the solar system stopped, all living organisms died with the exception of those inside the ark. Rav Mintz explains that the constant movement of the solar system cleans and purifies the air on Earth. The ark, however, insulated the people and animals from the stale air and, thus, they were able to survive.

When Noach sent out the raven, it immediately returned. This was due to the fact that the air was not yet moving outside, so the raven did not want to be there. By the time the dove was sent out, the weather was better, but was not yet 100 percent. Due to the imperfect air quality, the dove had to be brought back to the ark by Noach, but it did not need to come in right away. Finally, the dove was sent out again and returned with an olive branch, so Noach understood that it would now be safe to leave the ark.

Rav Mintz asks, Why did the raven need to come back right away while the dove needed to be brought back in by Noach? He explains that the difference is between a raven, a non-kosher, impure bird versus the dove, which is *tahor* ("pure") and kosher. The raven could not tolerate the stale air, as the solar system had not yet returned to full "power." The dove, on the other hand, was pure and kosher, so HaShem performed a miracle, allowing the dove to sustain itself despite the lack of good air movement and quality. The dove was able to exist outside of the ark just as it had existed the entire period of the *Mabul* inside the ark. In fact, the Torah goes out of its way to tell us that the *yonah*—the dove—could not find a place to rest its foot and therefore returned to the ark. The dove returned to the ark specifically because the water was still on the ground, *not* because the dove could not tolerate the air quality.

Perhaps we can derive from this teaching the lesson of the miracle of the constant movement of our solar system, our galaxy, and the entire universe...it never stops. In order for our world to exist and maintain itself, HaShem required it to be in a constant state of movement 365 days a year. The moment this movement stopped, the entire ecology broke down, creating havoc and devastation on the world.

The true servants of God are those who work around the clock, never stopping. If we want to become good servants to HaShem, then we need to be consistent in what we do. It is not enough just to try something a few times and hope that this will become intrinsic to our beings. We need to make a long-term commitment to whatever religious or mundane matter we want to tackle. The key to success is doing it for a long time. How long of a time should it take? We learn from a *mishnah* how long things take to settle in (*Bava Basra* 28a). The *mishnah* states that after a person resides in a property for three years without objection from the previous owner, he attains a *chazakah* and is no longer required to show a document as proof. The number three in Jewish law teaches *chazakah* ("halachic status of permanence or ownership") in many areas. I would therefore suggest that three years is about the right amount of time to try something out. After doing something for three years, our metabolism will finally take on this new commitment of the body and soul.

◆ ◆ ◆

There are times in life when a person is taken advantage of and made to feel both used and abused by another. There is no question that there are merits to the complaint, and being angry is totally valid. So we make up our mind to no longer have anything to do with the offending person in order to avoid running the risk of being taken advantage of again. In fact, it's probably a mitzvah to stay away in order to avoid additional discomfort and anger. The problem arises if a relative or a friend of the person who wronged us needs our help or assistance. Our initial reaction is probably to say no. We resolve not to help because of the risk of being used again by that same other person. But should our anger extend to refusing to help a fellow Jew in need simply because he is associated with the person who once took advantage of us?

The answer to this question is found in the Torah (*Devarim*:15:1–2): "*Mi'keitz sheva shanim taaseh Shemittah, v'zeh dvar ha'Shemitah; shamote kal baal mashei yado asher yisa b'reieihu lo yigos es reieihu v'es echav ki kara Shemittah laHashem—At the end of seven years you shall institute a remission. And this is the manner of remission: remit every creditor of a loan over what he wants to collect from his fellow. He shall not pressure his fellow or his brother, for He has proclaimed a remission for HaShem.*" The *Sefer HaChinuch*, in mitzvah 84, lists many reasons why the laws of *Shemittah* and forgoing loans are part and parcel of the Torah. Through the fulfillment of this mitzvah, we strengthen our *emunah* and *bitachon* in HaShem. By fulfilling these mitzvos, a person learns that money is not the most important thing in the world. But the *Chinuch* teaches us a far greater lesson: Through this mitzvah, a person acquires a character trait of *vatranus*—giving in to things and foregoing that which we want in order to stand on principle. It says that there is no greater *middah* to work on than giving in and letting things slide.

Rav Eliyahu Dessler in *Michtav Mi'Eliyahu* writes frequently about *middos* and character development. He states that the central core of all *middos* is the *middah* of *chesed*—kindness and feeling for the other person. In section 3, a powerful story is related from a Gemara in *Kesuvos* 104. The story is told about the great Rabbi Yehuda HaNasi, whose entire life was dedicated to the Jewish people through the organization of the entire Mishnah for everyone else's benefit. This was an enormous *chesed*. Rabbi Yehuda HaNasi, who was extraordinarily wealthy, had a table that was always full of delicacies, yet he never partook of any of them. Those treats were meant only for his guests. The Gemara records that when Rabbi Yehuda HaNasi died, his ten fingers pointed toward heaven and he stated that "my ten fingers were only used for Torah; I never benefited with even my small pinky."

In contrast, in *Bava Metzia* 85, a calf was on its way to slaughter when it buried its face in Rabbi Yehuda HaNasi's cloak and cried. He then said to the calf, "This is the purpose for which you were created." Rabbi Yehuda HaNasi knew through *ruach ha'kodesh* that a great Torah scholar would eat and benefit from this sacrifice. It was said in heaven that since Rebbi (as he was called) did not show compassion for the animal just that one time, he would have to endure hardships in the future. From his perspective, there was no cruelty or intention to insult the animal with his statement. Nevertheless, there was a minute trace of insensitivity even though the animal knew it was going to serve HaShem in its way. The calf still found it difficult to give up its life— even for the sake of God.

A person can be selfless and full of compassion, and yet think he can rightfully decide to ignore someone in his time of need. We learn from these two Gemaras that even when a person thinks that he has a right to be angry or annoyed with someone, he has to control his anger and rise above it. He has to focus on what God expects of him under these circumstances.

This is all easier said than done. In order for a person to overcome legitimate feelings of anger and hurt regarding another person, he must always strengthen himself through doing more and more kindness. One must realize that the *chesed* that is not done is an insult to the Creator, because HaShem would never turn down a request just because He was angry from another previous and unrelated situation.

We all take advantage of HaShem's kindness and do not always live up to His expectations, and despite that fact, we are not ashamed to go back and ask for more assistance. In order to become great, we must emulate God in this regard and work on our *middos*, even when it goes against our grain.

◆　◆　◆

As a pulpit rabbi, teacher, and educator, I have always looked for the secret to success with regards to the learning styles and needs of children and adults. Success strengthens a person's self-confidence— whether child or adult—leading to less stress and better mental health. In today's world, children, in particular (adults had these same issues when they were children, now they have just grown up physically, but have retained some of the same problems), face many challenges in life which can be overpowering, scary, and downright ugly. Children develop insecurity and sometimes inferiority complexes that may paralyze them in the short term, but can have everlasting effects throughout their lives.

Many of our children today lack confidence. I believe that is the reason why so many people are enamored with athletes, entertainers, politicians, and the like. These celebrities tend to show exuberance, control, poise, and a certain coolness. These public figures display a seeming self-assurance which, even when they mess up on the field or on stage, enables them to bounce right back up and move forward. They play and confront the opposition without any display of fear or nerves. Although there is an element of deception here, nevertheless, the genuine success and confidence displayed may very well be drawing on a childhood that built their confidence through accomplishment.

I remember building model airplanes and ships (my favorite was the aircraft carrier) as a child. I recall pulling all the pieces off the plastic attachment and laying them all out. With that great smelling cement, I would happily and carefully glue each of the pieces together. Slowly, but surely, as every day passed and a few more parts were added, the model took form right before my eyes. I cannot recall what happened to all those models, but I remember being so proud after each one was completed.

Unfortunately, today, electronics dominate the kids' world. This is not to say there is not or cannot be stimulation of the brain and hand-eye coordination. Nevertheless, at the end of the day, having something tangible to show for their hard work is not out there for all to see.

The Torah spends much time dedicated to the construction and building of the Mishkan ("the portable Temple") and its contents. In addition, we read about the clothing of the *Kohen* and the *Kohen Gadol*, which had to be worn during the services performed in the Mishkan. The Torah describes the wood used for the Mishkan. In *parashas Terumah* (*Shemos* 26:15) it states: "*V'asisa es ha'kerashim la'Mishkan, atzei shittim omdim—You shall make the beams of the Mishkan of shittim wood, standing erect.*" The Midrash explains the word *omdim* ("standing erect"), as standing forever—for eternity.

The Ksav Sofer explains that everything in the world has something above it. From the ground sprouts forth vegetation, and from the vegetation, a higher level is life (as in animal life). At the highest level is the human being, who is alive and can speak. Trees that bear fruit maintain a certain dignity and importance because of the fruit they provide. Animals and human beings can take and use the fruit of that tree, thereby giving the tree an important position in the world. On the other hand, the *atzei shittim*—the *shittim* trees—do not produce any fruit to give it significance. These *shittim* trees remain there standing in the same way throughout their entire existence. Therefore, God commanded us to take this particular wood for the Tabernacle that would house the presence of HaShem. The wood retained its simplicity and therefore was taken to be used in the holiness of the building. Because the *shittim* tree provided the wood necessary for building the walls of the Mishkan, its very simplicity in strength and beauty gave it lasting importance.

How can we contrast the using of simple wood to build the sanctuary of God to the building of models? Consider the famous words: "*To make Me a sanctuary that I may dwell in you*" (*Shemos* 25:8). God is commanding us to build a sanctuary for Him, but in reality it is really for us—to become close to HaShem. The Rabbis have often said that we are the sanctuary, and we need to become the receptacle to allow God's Presence to dwell within each of us! HaShem commanded the Jewish people to build a building for Him to dwell in and this act of building lifted the spirits of the entire Jewish people. The Mishkan atoned for the sin of the Golden Calf. Building the Mishkan corrected the wrongs of the Jewish people, returning their confidence (that they are the Chosen People and are back in the good grace of God) and their glory. Taking the mundane, building and fashioning it into something tangible, something from which we can feel both pride and a sense of accomplishment, is an act which emulates the ways of HaShem. HaShem dwells among us when we emulate His ways, when we look at the mundane, common objects which surround us and make them into something beautiful and special.

If children and adults become constructive in any area, it makes them feel elevated, ultimately building their self-esteem and developing their confidence in undertaking bigger and better things in life. We all should take on a project of building, painting, learning to play an instrument, crocheting, or anything else we have a talent for. As we accomplish, we will grow, and as we grow, we will want to continue to achieve and to succeed. The Torah sends to each of us this powerful and beautiful lesson: we are all capable of experiencing continuous growth, that vibrant, internal creative force which, in turn, feeds us to accomplish even more. Ultimately, our service to HaShem will be enhanced with greater exuberance and joy.

Index of Torah Personalities

(A list of Torah personalities that I have either quoted or drawn from their teachings)

Abarbanel

Isaac ben Judah Abravanel (1437–1508) commonly referred to just as Abravanel, also spelled Abarbanel or Abrabanel, was a Portuguese Jewish statesman, philosopher, Torah commentator, and financier. Abravanel was born in Lisbon, Portugal. A student of the Rabbi of Lisbon, Joseph Chaim, he became well versed in rabbinic literature and in the learning of his time, devoting his early years to the study of Jewish philosophy. This attracted the attention of King Afonso V of Portugal who employed him as treasurer.

Alshich HaKadosh

Moshe Alshich (1508–1593), known as the Alshich Hakadosh (the Holy), was a prominent Rabbi, preacher, and Torah commentator in the latter part of the 16th century. He became a student of Rabbi Joseph Caro. His students included Rabbi Hayim Vital and Rabbi Yom Tov Tzahalon.

Apta Ruv

Avraham Yehoshua Heshel of Apt (1748–1825), popularly known as the Apter Rebbe or Apter Rov.

Rabbi Chaim ben Attar

Rabbi Chaim ben Attar was a Talmudist and kabbalist. He was one of the most prominent Rabbis of Morocco.

Avnei Nezer

Avrohom Bornsztain (1838–1910) was a leading *posek* in late-19th-century Europe and founder and first Rebbe of the Sochatchover Chasidic dynasty. He is known as the Avnei Nezer (Stones of the Crown) after the title of his posthumously published set of Torah responsa. Avrohom Bornsztain became a close *talmid* of the Kotzker Rebbe who chose him as his son-in-law. His only son, Shmuel, author of *Shem Mishmuel*, succeeded him as Rebbe.

Ba'al ha-Turim

Jacob ben Asher was an influential Medieval rabbinic authority. Known as Ba'al ha-Turim (Master of the Rows), after his main work in Halachah, the *Arba'ah Turim* (Four Rows). The work was divided into four sections each called a *"tur,"* alluding to the rows of jewels on the High Priest's breastplate.

The Bach

Rav Yoel Sirkes of Cracow (1561–1641), the Bach, was the author of *Bais Chadash* on the *Tur*, in which he traced each law to its source in the Gemara. He was the teacher and father-in-law of Rav Dovid HaLevy, the Taz.

Rabbeinu Bachya

Bahya ben Asher ibn Halawa, also known as Rabbeinu Behaye (1255–1340), was a Rabbi and scholar of Judaism. He was a commentator on the Torah.

He is considered by Jewish scholars to be one of the most distinguished of the Torah exegetes of Spain. He was a pupil of Rabbi Shlomo ben Aderet (the Rashba).

Beis Halevi

Yosef Dov Soloveitchik (1820–1892) was the author of *Beis Halevi*, by which name he is better known. He was the great-grandson of Rabbi Chaim Volozhin.

He composed works on Jewish law (responsa) called *Shu"t Beis Halevi*, as well as a commentary on the first book (*Bereishis*) and part of the second book (*Shemos*) of the Torah (*Beis Halevi al HaTorah*).

Ben Ish Chai

Yosef Chaim (1832–1909) was a leading Chacham (Sephardic Rabbi), authority on Jewish law (Halachah) and master kabbalist. He is best known as author of the work on Halachah, *Ben Ish Chai* (Son of Man Who Lives).

Moses Chagiz

Moses Chagiz (1671–1750) was a Talmudic scholar, Rabbi, kabbalist, and author born in Jerusalem, Palestine. He was one of the most prominent and influential Jewish leaders in seventeenth-century Amsterdam.

Chidushei HaRim

Yitzchak Meir Alter (1799–1866) is considered to be the first Rebbe of the Ger Chasidic dynasty which he founded in the town of Góra Kalwaria (known as "Ger" in Yiddish), Poland. He was also known as the Chidushei HaRim for his Torah *sefarim*.

Rav Meir Chodosh

Rav Meir Chodosh (1898–1989) was *mashgiach* of Yeshivas Chevron, Ateres Yisrael, and Ohr Elchanan. Born in Lithuania, he was a talmid *muvhak* of the Alter of Slabodka, Rav Nosson Tzvi Finkel.

Rav Eliyahu Eliezer Dessler

Rav Dessler (1892–1953) was a Rabbi, Talmudic scholar, and Jewish philosopher of the 20th century. He was known as *mashgiach ruchani* (spiritual counselor) of the Ponevezh yeshiva in Israel. Eliyahu Dessler was a disciple of one of the main leaders of the Mussar Movement, Rabbi Simcha Zissel Ziv, best known as the Alter (Elder) of Kelm. His students edited his collected correspondence and ethical writings posthumously in the six-volume *Michtav me-Eliyahu* (Letter from Eliyahu) which alludes to the letter that the prophet Eliyahu sent to the King of Yehudah that arrived after Eliyahu ascended to

Heaven in a chariot of fire, later translated into English and published as *Strive for Truth*.

Ein Yaakov

In 1492, when the Jews were expelled from Spain, Jacob Ibn Habib settled in Salonica, where he wrote his *En Yaakob* in the house of Don Judah ben Abraham Benveniste.

Rabbi Herman Gross

Rabbi Herman Gross was a businessman, inventor, and learned layman, author of two *sefarim*, *Nachlas Tzvi* and *Ateres Tzvi*. He was born in Hungary in 1863. Gross immigrated to the United States in 1893 and after World War I, the family moved to Boro Park, Brooklyn. He viewed his business solely as a means of subsistence, for his true passion was Torah. He retired from business at a relatively young age to devote himself to Torah study and was supported by his sons.

Imrei Chaim

Rabbi Chaim Meir of Vizhnitz (1888–1972), popularly known as the Imrei Chaim, was a direct descendant of Rabbi Menachem Mendel Hager of Kossov.

Eliyahu Kitov

Avraham Eliyahu Mokotow (1912–1976), better known as Eliyahu Kitov, was a Rabbi, educator, and community activist. He was born in Warsaw, Poland as Avraham Eliyahu Mokotowski. *Sefer HaToda'ah*, his most famous work, was translated into English by Rabbi Nachman Bulman as *The Book of Our Heritage*.

Kli Yakar

Shlomo Ephraim ben Aaron Luntschitz was a Rabbi, poet, and Torah commentator, best known for his Torah commentary *Kli Yakar*. He served as the Rabbi of Prague from 1604–1619.

Rabbi Yisrael Be'eri Kolodner

Rabbi Yisrael Be'eri Kolodner was born in 1911 in Drohitchin. In 1943, Rav Yisrael was appointed a Rabbi in the old colony of Nes Ziona, where he excelled in various areas. He taught Talmud to elderly men and was concerned with the education of children; he founded a charity fund for residents of the colony, and created a charity fund for visitors. He also assisted new immigrants to find places to live.

Rebbe Yechezkel Taub of Kuzmir

Rebbe Yechezkel Taub of Kuzmir (1755–1856) established yeshivas and a type of Chasidic teaching that was similar to that of his rebbes, the Seer of Lublin and the Kozhnitzer Magid. His son, Rebbe Shmuel Eliyahu Taub of Zvolin, Poland, succeeded him, excelling in Torah scholarship and in creating Chasidic songs. He was called *menagen mafli pla'os*, Hebrew for "a wondrous musical talent." His first son, Rabbi Moshe Aharon, succeeded him, while his second son, Rebbe Yisrael, went on to found the actual Modzitz Chasidic dynasty.

Maharal

Judah Loew ben Bezalel (1520–1609), widely known as the Maharal of Prague, or simply the Maharal, which is the Hebrew acronym of "**M**oreinu **HaR**av **L**oew" (our teacher Rabbi Loew), was a renowned Talmudic scholar, Jewish mystic, and philosopher who, for most of his life, served as a leading Rabbi in the cities of Mikulov in Moravia and Prague in Bohemia. Among his great works is *Gur Aryeh al HaTorah*, a supercommentary on Rashi's Torah commentary. The Maharal is the subject of a 19th-century legend that he created the Golem of Prague, an animate being fashioned from clay.

The Maharsha

Rabbi Samuel Eidels (1555–1631) was a renowned Rabbi and Talmudist famous for his commentary on the Talmud, *Chiddushei Halachot*. Eidels is commonly known as the Maharsha, a Hebrew acronym for "**M**oreinu **HaR**av **Sh**muel **E**idels" (our teacher Rabbi Shmuel Eidels).

The Malbim

Meïr Leibush ben Yechiel Michel Weiser, better known by the acronym Malbim, was a 19th-century Rabbi, Hebrew grammar master, and Torah commentator.

Rabbi Reuvein Margoles

Rabbi Reuvein Margolies was born in 1889 in Lemberg. He was a prolific writer on many Jewish topics. He emigrated to Israel in 1934, settling in Tel-Aviv.

Rabbi Shalom Mashash

Rabbi Mashash served as Jerusalem's Chief Rabbi for 25 years. He was appointed Chief Rabbi of Casablanca in the year 1949, and later served as Chief Rabbi of Morocco.

Meiri

Rabbi Menachem ben Solomon Meiri was a provincial scholar and commentator of the Talmud. He summarized the teachings of his predecessors of the previous three centuries.

Meshech Chochma

Meir Simcha of Dvinsk (1843–1926) was a Rabbi and prominent leader of Judaism in Eastern Europe in the early 20th century. He was a Kohen, and is therefore often referred to as Meir Simcha ha-Kohen. He is known for his writings on Maimonides' Mishneh Torah, which he titled *Ohr Somayach,* as well as his *chidushim* on the Torah, titled *Meshech Chochma.*

Reb Moshe

Rav Moshe Feinstein (1895–1986) was a Lithuanian Orthodox Rabbi, scholar and *posek* (an authoritative adjudicator of questions related to Jewish law), who was world-renowned for his expertise in Halachah and was regarded by many as the de facto supreme halachic authority for Jewry of North America during his lifetime. He is widely referred to simply as Reb Moshe, and his halachic rulings are widely quoted in contemporary rabbinic literature.

Netziv

Naftali Zvi Yehuda Berlin (1816–1893), commonly known by the acronym Netziv, was a Rabbi, Rosh Yeshiva of the Volozhin Yeshiva, and author of several works of rabbinic literature in Lithuania.

Noam Elimelech

Elimelech Weisblum of Lizhensk (1717–1787) was one of the great founding Rebbes of the Chasidic movement. Rebbi Elimelech authored the classic work *Noam Elimelech*. This work developed the Chasidic theory of the Tzaddik.

Ohr ha-Chaim

Chaim ben Moses ibn Attar (1696–1743) also known as the Ohr ha-Chaim, after his popular commentary on the Torah, was a Talmudist and kabbalist. He was born in Mequenez, Morocco, and was one of their most prominent Rabbis.

Rambam

Moshe ben Maimon, acronym for "**R**abbeinu **M**oshe **B**en **M**aimon" (our Rabbi/teacher Moses son of Maimon), a preeminent medieval Sephardic Jewish philosopher and astronomer, became one of the most prolific and influential Torah scholars of the Middle Ages, as well as a renowned physician. Born in Córdoba (present-day Spain) on Passover Eve, 1135 or 1138, he died in Egypt on December 12, 1204, whence his body was taken to the lower Galilee and buried in Tiberias.   His fourteen-volume *Mishneh Torah* carries significant authority as a codification of Talmudic law.

The Ran

Nissim ben Reuven (1320–1376) of Girona, Catalonia was an influential Talmudist and authority on Jewish law. He was one of the last of the great Spanish medieval Talmudic scholars. He is known as the Ran, the Hebrew acronym of his name, as well as the Ranbar, the Hebrew acronym of his full name, including his father's name, Reuvein. His best-known work is his commentary and explanation of Rav Alfasi's *Hilkhot*, which had, at that time, been adopted for practical decisions.

Rashbam

Shmuel ben Meir (1085–1158), known best as the Rashbam, a Hebrew acronym for "**R**abbi **S**hmuel **B**en **M**eir," was a leading French Tosafist and grandson of Shlomo Yitzhaki (Rashi). He was born in the vicinity of Troyes, France to his father, Meir ben Shmuel, and mother,

Yocheved, daughter of Rashi. He was the older brother of the Tosafists Isaac ben Meir (the Rivam) and Jacob ben Meir (Rabbeinu Tam), and a colleague of Rabbi Joseph Kara. Like his maternal grandfather, the Rashbam was a Torah commentator and Talmudist. He learned from Rashi and from Isaac ben Asher ha-Levi (Riva).

Rabbi Yitzchok Reitbard

Rav Yitzchok Ben Nissan lived sometime in the late 1800s in the town of Yanava which was close to the city of Pinsk. He authored *Sefer Kehillas Yitzchok* on the *parshios* of the Torah. He was a disciple of Rav Yosef Dov Halevi Soloveitchik, the Av Beis Din of Brisk and well known as the Beis Halevi.

Sfas Emes

Yehudah Aryeh Leib Alter (1847–1905), also known by the title of his main work, the Sfas Emes, was a Chasidic Rabbi who succeeded his grandfather, Rabbi Yitzchak Meir Alter, as the av beis din (head of the rabbinical court) and Rav of Góra Kalwaria, Poland (known in Yiddish as the town of Ger). He succeeded the Rebbe, Reb Heynekh of Alexander, as Rebbe of the Gerrer Chasidim.

Sforno

Obadiah ben Jacob Sforno was an Italian Rabbi, philosopher, and physician. He is best known for his masterful commentary on the Torah.

Rabbi Meir Shapiro

Rabbi Meir Shapiro founded the revolutionary idea of Daf Yomi, a daily regimen of studying the Babylonian Talmud one *daf* each day. Under this regimen, the entire Talmud is completed, one day at a time, in a cycle of seven-and-a-half years.

Shelah HaKadosh

Isaiah Horowitz was born in Prague around 1565, a disciple of Moses Isserles (Rema). His most important work *Shenei Luchot HaBerit* (Two Tablets of the Covenant: abbreviated *Shelah*), is an encyclopedic compilation of ritual, ethics, and mysticism.

Rav Menachem ben Shlomo

Rav Menachem ben Shlomo was born in Italy in the 12th century He was a grammarian and he authored Midrash Seichel Tov. It is a collection of old Midrashic material, arranged on each verse of the Torah and the five Megillos. It is interspersed with halachic notes and original comments.

Rav Moshe Shternbuch

Rav Moshe Shternbuch is the Vice President of the Rabbinical Court and Ra'avad of the Edah HaChareidis in Jerusalem. He resides in Har Nof where he is the Rabbi of the local Gra Synagogue, named after the Vilna Gaon of whom he is a direct descendant.

Skverer Rebbe

Rabbi David Twersky (born October 28, 1940) is the Grand Rabbi and spiritual leader of the village of New Square, New York and of Skverer Chasidism worldwide.

Rabbi Shimon Sofer

Rabbi Shimon Sofer (1850–1944) was the progenitor of the Erlau Chasidic dynasty. He was the son of Rabbi Shmuel Benyamin Sofer, known as the Ksav Sofer, and grandson of Rabbi Moses Sofer, the Chasam Sofer. Rabbi Shimon Sofer authored two *sefarim*, the *Hisorerus Tshuva Responsa* and *Shir Maon*. Hence he is known to many simply as the Hisorerus Tshuva. In all, Rabbi Shimon Sofer led the Jewish community in Erlau for some 64 years.

Yitzchak Elchanan Spektor

Rav Yitzchak Elchanan Spektor (1817–1896) was a renowned *posek* and Talmudic sage of the 19th century.

Targum Yonasan

Yonasan ben Uzziel is known as the author of Targum Yonasan. He is also said to have written a book of kabbalah known as Megadnim. He was one of the 80 Tannaim who studied under Hillel the Elder. Yonasan ben Uzziel's tomb is in Amuka, Galilee, near Tzfat, Israel. Traditionally, those who are unmarried visit this location seeking to be granted blessings in his honor, and in his merit find a marriage partner.

Rav Yisrael Eliyahu Yehoshua Trunk

Rav Trunk (1821–1893), born in Plotsk, published several *sefarim*, including *Yeshuas Yisrael* on *Choshen Mishpat*, *Yeshuos Malko*, and *Yavin Daas*.

Rabbi Yaakov Tzvi

Rabbi Yaakov Tzvi was born in 1785 in Lissa, Germany. This city was renowned as a center of Torah scholarship, as well as for its great *Rabbanim*.

The Vilna Gaon

Eliyahu ben Shlomo Zalman Kremer (1720–1797), known as the Vilna Gaon or Eliyahu of Vilna, or by his Hebrew acronym Gra ("**G**aon **R**abbenu **E**liyahu"), was a Talmudist, halachist, kabbalist, and one of the foremost leaders of Jewry of the past few centuries. He is commonly referred to in Hebrew as *haGaon haChasid miVilna* (the saintly genius from Vilnius).

Rav Menachem Mendel of Vishiva

Rav Menachem Mendel (ben Yisrael) of Vishiva (1886–1941), author of the *She'eris Menachem*. Born as the oldest son of the Vizhnitzer Rebbe, he founded the Yeshiva Beis Yisrael and was appointed Rav in Vizhnitz by the time he was 25 years old. In 1922, he was appointed Rav in Vishiva.

Rebbe Meir Yechiel

Rebbe Meir Yechiel was a *talmid* of Rebbe Elimelech of Grodzisk, a scion of the Kozhnitzer dynasty (and father of the Piaseczno Rebbe). After the *petirah* (passing) of Rebbe Elimelech, many Chasidim accepted Rebbe Meir Yechiel as their Rebbe, and thus the Ostrovtza dynasty was born.

Supporters

Beth Jacob Congregation, San Diego
BSBI Congregation, Chas. S.C.
Buddy and Rivka Berkowitz
Yakov, z"l, and Ava Bogopulsky and Family
Andrew and Shauna Breskin
Maxwell and Deborah Brookler
Drs. Esomer and Devorah Brim and Family
Erez and Eva Burg
Dr. Ron and Mollie Caplan
Pinny and Pam Dollman
Yitz and Yaffy Dyckman and Family
Richard and Julie Goodwin
Meir and Itta Graff
Alan and Elisheva Green
Allen and Toni Gruber
Hillel Academy, Binghamton N.Y.
Ari and Esther Jacobs and Family
Doris Jaffe
Leopold and Marilyn Kahn
Eli and Debbie Kaplan
Yaacov and Yehudis Kaplan
Rabbi Asher and Ruchie Klein
Yaakov and Shanna Klein
Glenn and Natalie Kornfeld
Shmuel and Elisheva Kovacs and Family
Max Landau
Marty and Leah Mally
Norm and Rona Orgel
Kay Raffie Pekin
Steven and Lee Polinsky
Robert and Claire Sigal
Dovid and Bashi Simon
Joel and Faye Snyder
Chaim and Alyssa Winter
Zvi and Stephanie Zauderer

About the Author

Avraham Bogopulsky has been the rabbi of Beth Jacob Congregation in San Diego for the past twenty years. Born and raised in New York, he received his bachelor's degree in psychology from St. Thomas Aquinas and his *semichah* from Rabbi Berel Wein. He continues to maintain a close *rebbi/talmid* relationship with Rabbi Leibel Reznick.

Rabbi Bogopulsky is involved with every part of the Jewish community in San Diego. He teaches at the local yeshiva high schools for both girls and boys. He maintains the current *eruv* in San Diego and administers the *kashrus* agency of the local Vaad. In addition, he provides pastoral care and leads the life-cycle events of his shul and community.

Rabbi Bogopulsky and his wife Leah raised five children in warm and sunny San Diego, who have since grown up, married, and live in different communities in the United States and Israel.

About
Mosaica Press

Mosaica Press is an independent publisher of Jewish books. Our authors include some of the most profound, interesting, and entertaining thinkers and writers in the Jewish community today. There is a great demand for high-quality Jewish works dealing with issues of the day — and Mosaica Press is helping fill that need. Our books are available around the world. Please visit us at www. mosaicapress.com or contact us at info@mosaicapress.com. We will be glad to hear from you